Liturgical Inculturation:

Sacramentals, Religiosity, and Catechesis

Liturgical Inculturation:

Sacramentals, Religiosity, and Catechesis

Anscar J. Chupungco, O.S.B.

A PUEBLO BOOK

The Liturgical Press Collegeville, Minnesota

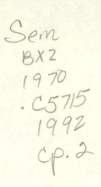

A Pueblo book published by The Liturgical Press

Design by Frank Kacmarcik

Library of Congress Cataloging-in-Publication Data

Chupungco, Anscar J.
    Liturgical inculturation : sacramentals, religiosity, and catechesis / Anscar J. Chupungco.
       p.   cm.
    "A Pueblo book."
    Includes bibliographical references.
    ISBN 0-8146-6120-3
    1. Catholic Church—Liturgy. 2. Christianity and culture.
3. Sacramentals. 4. Catechetics—Catholic Church. 5. Catholic Church—Education.   I. Title.
BX1970.C5715   1992
264'.02—dc20   92–13808
                                                CIP

To Dom Adrian Nocent, O.S.B.

Contents

Introduction

Inculturation as a branch of liturgical study has a fairly wide scope. It covers the areas of history and theology, liturgical and cultural principles, process and methods, sacraments and sacramentals, Liturgy of the Hours, liturgical year, liturgical music, liturgical arts and furnishings, and such related topics as popular religiosity and catechesis. The list is quite generic, for each of these topics has several aspects.

This volume, which is a sequel to *Liturgies of the Future: The Process and Methods of Inculturation* (Paulist Press, 1989), reviews the different technical terms expressing the relationship between liturgy and culture before proceeding to discuss the question of sacramentals, popular religiosity, and liturgical catechesis. Though the three topics are disparate, they share the same basic concern of inculturation. For sacramentals and catechesis to be relevant, they need to be inculturated. For the liturgy to relate to the religious experience of a large segment of the Church, it must interact with popular religiosity.

Throughout this book much stress is given to the question of method, with obvious partiality to dynamic equivalence. Inculturation is, strictly speaking, not creativity but the dynamic translation of the typical editions into the cultures of local Churches. Part of the method is to examine with great care what the typical editions allow, propose, and suggest, just as part of the method is to consider also what culture offers or requires. Inculturation works on existing realities in the Church and in the world. Inculturation does not, however, rule out creativity, which is the final phase of Vatican II's liturgical renewal. Creativity alone can fully satisfy all the spiritual and cultural needs of a local Church, though inculturation is still the best school where it is learned.

Several people have contributed to the content of this book. Foremost among them are my colleagues and students at the Pontifical

Liturgical Institute with whom I have had enriching discussions, not to say debates, on inculturation. Many more contributed during the open forum following the talks I have been privileged to deliver in various parts of the world. Their personal reactions, whether sympathetic or critical, have greatly influenced my thinking on the topics addressed in this book.

Like the previous books I have written on inculturation, the present one has surely its rough edges and loose ends. Since I started to give the course on liturgical adaptation at the Pontifical Liturgical Institute in 1973, I have always been keenly aware that the ground I tread on is full of uncertainties. It is with a sense of limitation that I offer this volume to fellow liturgists and students in the hope of stirring up fresh reflections on how best to make the liturgy alive and relevant to our time.

Chapter One

Preliminary Questions on Inculturation

A DEFINITION OF TERMS

Over the years different technical terms have been tried in liturgical circles in an attempt to express as accurately as possible the relationship between liturgy and culture. The more popular among them are "indigenization," "incarnation," "contextualization," "revision," "adaptation," "acculturation," and "inculturation." To describe how inculturation works, other technical terms such as "transculturation," "deculturation," and "exculturation" have subsequently been coined and entered into the active vocabulary of scholarly studies. Although it has become rather fashionable nowadays to use these technical terms, especially "inculturation," it is important to keep in mind that they are jargons. They belong to the peculiar terminology used on different occasions by anthropologists and borrowed gratefully by theologians, missiologists, and liturgists. To the uninitiated most of them are outlandish, if not linguistically barbarous.[1]

Each of these technical terms, when used of the liturgy, refers to a particular facet of the relationship between liturgy and culture. However, none is comprehensive enough to express the full spectrum of that relationship. They all convey the idea of interaction between two or more parties, but terms like "revision," "adaptation," and "contextualization" do not have immediate cultural underpinnings, whereas the term "incarnation" implies, at least in contemporary theological usage, some kind of a cultural exchange. There is no hard and fast definition of these terms, yet care should be taken not to use them synonymously lest they lose their proper nuance, thus making it difficult to detect their precise meaning or what the writer has in mind.

Not all of the above-mentioned terms are here to stay. In fact, "in-

---

1. *Webster's Ninth New Collegiate Dictionary* does not accept "indigenization," "contextualization," and "inculturation," although it enters "acculturation."

digenization" has altogether passed out of notice, while "incarnation" and "contextualization" no longer have the kind of popularity they once enjoyed. Nevertheless, it would be useful to clarify how they have been used in the past and how contemporary liturgical literature understands them.[2]

Indigenization. Coined from the word "indigenous," this term refers to the process of conferring on Christian liturgy a cultural form that is native to the local community. In the seventies D. S. Amalorpavadass advanced the use of this term in the liturgy. What he really meant was adaptation of the Christian liturgy in the framework of the culture of India. Indigenization, he explained, aims "to give to our liturgy a more Indian setting and complexion." For him "indigenization" was in fact another word for "Indianization."

The process, according to Amalorpavadass, has three phases. The first consists in creating an Indian setting for worship through the introduction of gestures, forms of homage, sacred objects, silence, and interiority, which are characteristic of Indian religious culture. The second consists in making adequate translations of the liturgy into the vernacular and eventually in composing new liturgical texts. The third consists in the reading of the sacred books of India, specifically the *Rig Veda,* as part of the Liturgy of the Word.[3]

Under the influence of Amalorpavadass, liturgists in the Philippines also used the term "indigenization." In the context of the seventies, which witnessed the revival in the Philippines of interest in the native cultural heritage, "indigenization" was taken to mean more than a mere synonym for "liturgical adaptation." It tried to further the people's appreciation of their cultural values and traditions. If in

---

2. For the elaboration of the terms "indigenization," "incarnation," and "contextualization" I am indebted to the unpublished licence thesis of N. Valle, "Adaptation and Related Terms in Missiological, Theological, and Liturgical Literature," which he presented to the Pontifical Liturgical Institute in 1989. His bibliography covers the years 1926–1989. See P. Schineller, *A Handbook on Inculturation* (New York, 1990) 14–27.

3. D. S. Amalorpavadass, *Towards Indigenisation in the Liturgy* (Bangalore, 1971) 26–53. The synod of bishops in 1974 discussed at some length the question of indigenization in the Church. See P. O'Connor, "The Bishops' Synod and Indigenization," *World Mission* 26 (1975) 4–12.

India "indigenization" meant "Indianization," in the Philippines it was another way of saying "Filipinization."

Indeed, Filipino Catholics have not known any form of official worship other than the Roman liturgy. Yet it continues to be a foreign element in the body of religious practices kept by the vast majority of the faithful. The reason for this was the inability of the liturgy, before Vatican II, to absorb indigenous traditions. Even during its baroque period the liturgy ignored the existence of native Filipino cultural expressions, though these possessed characteristics quite similar to the baroque. A need was felt in the seventies to incorporate native values and traditions into the texts and rites of official worship in order to bring the Roman liturgy closer to the cultural experience of Filipino worshipers. "Indigenization" was taken to mean the process of integrating the existing Western form of worship with the indigenous elements that made up the Filipino culture. Earlier, a similar process of integration had taken place when native practices assimilated elements of Christian worship to produce forms of popular religiosity, which at that time some liturgists enthusiastically called "folk liturgies."[4]

In the area of liturgical music a significant attempt was made in the Philippines as early as the sixties by B. Maramba, who composed music for the Ordinary of the Mass. The work, which carried the title *Pilipino Chant*, was published in a number of languages. The peculiar trait of Maramba's composition is its use of the indigenous rhythm and melodies of the Ifugao, Kalinga, and Maranaw tribes. As one could reasonably expect, this pioneering work sounded quaint to the lowland congregations, who are generally more attuned to Western music.[5] From the start the question that vexed liturgists in the Philippines was whether the concept and understanding of culture should

4. A. Chupungco, *Towards a Filipino Liturgy* (Quezon City, 1976) 47–95; idem: "A Filipino Attempt at Liturgical Inculturation," *Ephemerides liturgicae* 91/4–5 (1977) 370–376.

5. *The Pilipino Chant* was published in 1965 by the Benedictine Abbey of Manila in English, Tagalog, Cebuano, Bicol, Hiligaynon, Pampango, and Pangasinan. Maramba notes about his work that "the music of the Pilipino Chant has been predetermined, as it were, by the typical accents and stresses of the native Philippine languages. . . . The rhythm of the chant depends not on the note values but on speech patterns." See *Misa nga Pilipino sa Hiligaynon* (Manila, 1965) 2.

15

be confined to what is indigenous. Would not the retrieval of an indigenous form of music alienate the liturgy from contemporary cultural expression? We know that culture is incessantly subjected to evolution because of its inner dynamism and that it is continually enriched, and perhaps also impoverished, because of interaction with other cultures. At any rate, should not the contemporary phase of culture be the cutoff point and hence the point of departure for the process of liturgical renewal in the country?

In the seventies the term "indigenization" expressed local attempts to adapt the liturgy to what was perceived to be the native or indigenous elements of the people's culture. In some way it advanced the vague idea of a native liturgy. However, both etymologically and literally, this term represents an impossibility. Something is indigenous when it originates in or is produced, grows, and lives naturally in its own region or environment. In this sense, nothing can be made native or indigenous in foreign soil. Hence an indigenized Christian liturgy is an impossibility, and an indigenous form of worship is possible only in the land of its origin. What Pope John Paul II affirms regarding the gospel message surely applies to the liturgy: "It does not spring spontaneously from any cultural soil; it has always been transmitted by means of an apostolic dialogue which inevitably becomes part of a certain dialogue of cultures."[6] The liturgy is made up of essential elements that have been divinely instituted; these are transmitted through apostolic preaching. Though the liturgy has successfully been grafted onto cultures outside its origin, it has not thereby become indigenous to any of them.

Another difficulty presented by the term "indigenization" is the question of determining which elements constitute indigenous culture. How many nations in the world today can claim to be in possession of a culture that has no admixture of other cultures? The question is particularly relevant to multicultural countries like the United States. Though it has an indigenous community, it is a crossroads of ethnic groups from every region of the world. Its constitutive principle, *e pluribus unum*, has created the unusual phenomenon of a truly multiethnic nation wherein the indigenous Indian culture

6. John Paul II, *Catechesi tradendae*, 7, no. 53. English text in C. Bonivento, ed., *Going, Teach . . .* (Boston, 1980) 667. Henceforth *GT.*

does not constitute the substratum of the entire civilization. An indigenized liturgy in the United States, if that were at all possible, would, in effect, exclude all the other ethnic communities.

Besides the practical difficulty of defining what is indigenous, there is also the risk of creating a liturgy that is of interest to historians of culture but not to the liturgical assembly as a whole. Reversal to the indigenous form of culture or to an ancestral type smacks of archaeology and romanticism. We know that cultures are in a continual process of change due to mutual influence encouraged by modern means of communications. A culture cannot be defined without giving due regard to its newly acquired ingredients. It is obvious that indigenous culture, if this is no longer extant, cannot be the point of encounter between liturgy and culture. Since the liturgy is a living expression of faith, its cultural elements, with the exception of those that are of divine institution, should likewise be contemporary. The term "indigenization" can create the wrong impression that the liturgy is under the supervision of historians and museum curators.

Incarnation. Vatican II's decree *Ad gentes* inspired liturgical writers to refer to adaptation as "incarnation." Article 22 of the decree speaks of Christ's incarnation as the paradigm for the young Churches: "So too, just as happened in the economy of the incarnation [*ad instar oeconomiae incarnationis*], the young churches, which are rooted in Christ and built on the foundation of the apostles, acquire by a wondrous exchange all the riches of the nations which have been given to Christ as an inheritance." The idea is present also in *Ad gentes* 10: "If the church is to be in a position to offer to all the mystery of salvation and the life brought by God, then it must implant itself among every group of people in the same way that Christ by his incarnation committed himself to the particular social and cultural circumstances of the people among whom he lived."

The phrase *ad instar oeconomiae incarnationis* indicates that the conciliar decree sets Christ's incarnation as an exemplar to be copied faithfully. In imitation of Christ, who by virtue of the incarnation made himself one with the Jewish nation, the local Church should strive to identify itself with the people among whom it dwells. As Christ became a Jew in all things save sin, so the Church should become not merely a Church *in* but the Church *of* a particular locality.

17

The incarnation of the local Church inevitably affects the liturgy, which will likewise implant itself in the traditions and culture of every people. One may contend that the process of the Church's incarnation will attain completion when the liturgy shall have embodied in its rites and texts the people's cultural expressions.

Whenever incarnation is mentioned in connection with inculturation, there are liturgists who, in the spirit of the rediscovered paschal mystery, automatically append the resurrection. E. Kilmartin goes so far as to say that "the prime analogue of inculturation is the incarnation, life, death and glorification of Jesus Christ."[7] The statement is true, but it needs to be nuanced. The mystery of Christ's resurrection is not a paradigm of inculturation; unlike the mystery of the incarnation, it cannot be imitated. However, it is the underlying motive for why the liturgy should be incarnated: in order that the presence of the risen Christ, who is now seated at the right hand of God, may continue to be experienced in the Church.

The phrase "incarnation of the liturgy" is sometimes used as an equivalent of "liturgical adaptation." But it would be more accurate to consider it the theological basis of, rather than a synonym for liturgical adaptation. "Incarnation," both as a Christian mystery and a technical term, enriches our understanding of adaptation. As a mystery, it explains why the Church and its liturgy should adapt themselves to the culture and traditions of the people. What took place when God became human and dwelt among us now takes place when the Church and its liturgy embody "the riches of the nations." As a technical term, "incarnation" gives depth to adaptation, which is often simply understood as a work of external adjustment to or conformity with a situation. The liturgy is not merely adapted; it is, as it were, hypostatically united with the traditions and culture of the local Church. In short, it is incarnated.

After the council a good number of liturgists, among them C. Braga and I. Omaecheverria, elaborated on the relation of incarnation and adaptation.[8] There is an ongoing debate on the appropriateness

7. E. Kilmartin, "Culture and the Praying Church," *Canadian Studies in Liturgy* 5 (1990) 62.

8. C. Braga, "Un problema fondamentale di pastorale liturgica: adattamento e incarnazione nelle varie culture," *Ephemerides liturgicae* 89 (1975) 5–39; I.

or even propriety of using "incarnation" as a synonym for "adaptation." Those who prefer to speak of adaptation as incarnation argue that, unlike "adaptation," "incarnation" does not convey the idea of external imposition. "Incarnation" implies that the liturgical forms develop from the experience of the local Church.[9] There are, however, writers who, out of reverence for the mystery of Christ's incarnation, object to the wider use of the term. "Incarnation" is a technical term that should be set aside to express the unique mystery of God, who took our human nature. In support of this opinion, we make the observation that the decree *Ad gentes* phrases its doctrine carefully by referring to the incarnation of Christ as the pattern of encounter between the Church and culture. It does not speak of this encounter as an incarnation.

Contextualization. This term was introduced into the active vocabulary of the Church in 1972 by the World Council of Churches.[10] Derived from the word "contextual," it fittingly expresses the need for the Church to be relevant. The life and the mission of the Church will be relevant on condition that they relate to contemporary society. The environment and setting in which the local Church lives are the contexts that shed light on its theology, sacramental life, and missionary activity. The term distinctly echoes Vatican II's call for relevance, which it voiced in its constitution *Gaudium et spes.* This pastoral constitution seeks to set forth the relation of the Church to the modern world.

Since in some parts of the world human oppression is the dominant feature of daily life, the context in which the local Church lives and works is deeply affected by the struggle for political, economic,

Omaecheverria, "The Dogma of the Incarnation and the Adaptation of the Church to Various Peoples," *Omnis terra* 73 (1976) 277–283. See also A. Chupungco, *Cultural Adaptation of the Liturgy* (New York, 1982) 58–62; G. Brambilla, "Ermeneutica teologica dell'adattamento liturgico," *Liturgia e adattamento* (Rome, 1990) 39–83, esp. 54–71; D. S. Amalorpavadass, "Theological Reflections on Inculturation," *Studia liturgica* 20/1 (1990) 36–54.

9. R. Ramirez, "Liturgy from the Mexican American Perspective," *Worship* 51 (1977) 293–298.

10. R. Costa, *One Faith, Many Cultures: Inculturation, Indigenization, and Contextualization* (New York, 1988).

and cultural freedom. In such places "contextualization" is used to signify efforts toward liberation. This explains why the term has gained popularity in places where the theology of liberation and hope has taken root because of concern for material progress, social justice, and political liberty. Contextualization is thus an agenda that calls for immediate and resolute action. It invites the Church to review its social institutions in the context of the human aspirations of freedom and progress and to give full support to those who struggle justly to achieve them.[11]

In situations of political and economic oppression the local Church's liturgy inevitably yields to the demands of contextualized theological reflection. This will be noted especially in schools where students are actively involved in sociopolitical issues as well as in basic Christian communities that grapple with the problems of poverty and injustice. In such schools and communities the liturgy has sometimes been turned into a forum dramatizing the plight of the oppressed and the poor. Contextualized liturgies use symbols that have become a familiar sight during street rallies and demonstrations. In the seventies, the Church in the Philippines, then under martial law, witnessed a surge of creative liturgies that adopted the slogans, gestures, placards, and red banners used by activist groups to voice protest.

Contextualized liturgies adopt also the language of protest meant to excite anger or induce decisive action. Words like struggle are prominent in Marxist lexicon, while phrases like lifting up the lowly are of biblical origin. Typical of contextualized liturgies is the following intention for the prayer of the faithful, composed in the seventies: "For the powerful and influential on earth: preserve them from false ideologies and from hunger for power; give them prudence to avoid wars and promote peace." The following intention is likewise typical: "That the Church in our country may no longer be identified financially with the rich, socially with the powerful, and politically with the oppressors."[12] This forceful type of language, short of being

11. In the field of missiology, L. Luzbetak uses "contextualization" to express the relationship between culture and theology. See his article "Signs of Progress in Contextual Theology," *Verbum SVD* 22 (1981) 39–57.
12. *100 Prayers of the Faithful* (Manila, 1972) no. 8, p. 16; no. 21, p. 25.

inflammatory, points an accusing finger at the Church and people who hold power. In a sense, contextualization is allied with Christianity's prophetic role.[13] Through contextualization, the ideals of liberation theology gained access to the sacred confines of worship.

But contextualization is not a thing of the past. It represents the Church's continuing concern to be relevant to the contemporary world. At the same time, it suggests that worship should not be dissociated from the actual context of human life. D. Power is one who gives utterance to the timeliness of using contextualized language in the liturgy. Throughout his proposed alternative rite for the "ordination of a presbyter in a church constituted by basic Christian communities" we come across phrases that reveal the author's responsive attitude to the question of contextualization. Examples are: "God, giver and taker of life, your church is caught in the struggle to keep your very name alive"; "From among the weak and powerless of the world, you raise up to yourself prophets and teachers. In those who struggle for justice, you give your church its martyrs, witnesses to the truth and to divine love"; "Grant that he [the presbyter] may be inspired by the flame of love to share the people's struggle against injustice and to learn from their hope."[14]

Although contextualization is directly concerned with the situation of oppression and deprivation, it cannot be said to ignore the interaction that takes place between liturgy and culture. Context is a vibrant expression of human culture. If the liturgy is to be inculturated, it must also be contextualized. A. Stauffer has rightly pointed out that contextualization is part of the process of inculturation.[15]

Revision. This term is an important entry in the active vocabulary of the Constitution on the Liturgy, which on several occasions en-

13. P. Hiebert, "Critical Contextualization," *Missiology* 12 (1984) 287–296. See D. Hesselgrave and E. Rommen, *Contextualization. Meanings, Methods and Models* (Grand Rapids, 1989).

14. D. Power, "Alternative 1: Ordination of a Presbyter in a Church Constituted by Basic Christian Communities," *Alternative Futures for Worship*, 7 vols. (Collegeville, 1987) 6:157–164; also see his article "Liturgy and Empowerment," ibid., 81–104.

15. A. Stauffer, "Inculturation and Church Architecture," *Studia liturgica* 20/1 (1990) 70–80.

joins that the typical editions of the liturgical books should be revised in order to bring out more clearly the nature and purpose of the rites. The preconciliar liturgical movement, often called "classical" because of its marked predilection for the classical form of the Roman Rite, exerted a profound influence on the framers of the Constitution on the Liturgy. It should not come as a surprise that the conciliar document has strictly followed the blueprint of classical reform. *SC* 34 articulates this revisionist principle in these words: "The rites should be marked by a noble simplicity; they should be short, clear and unencumbered by useless repetitions; they should be within the people's power of comprehension and as a rule not require much explanation."

Revision suggests that the liturgical books, in this case the Tridentine books, are looked over again in order to correct, amend, improve, or update them. It would be useful to clarify two things in this regard. First, revision works on existing books. The council did not envision completely new typical editions of the liturgical books, except where they did not previously exist. Second, the work of revision follows the classical model. In this sense the revision of the typical editions is a type of restoration. During the council those who proposed classical restoration were taken to task by some council Fathers for seemingly advocating antiquated or obsolete models. Judging from the context in which the term "revision" was being used, there appeared to be a contradiction between revision as a means of *aggiornamento* and the classical restoration of the Roman liturgy.[16]

However, what the framers of the Constitution had in mind was to offer to local Churches a liturgical model, a typical edition, marked by the *sobrietas romana*. In this way they can more easily adapt the liturgical books to their culture after the example of the Franco-Germanic Churches in the eighth century. Hence, the term "revision," as used by the Constitution on the Liturgy, refers to the postconciliar and preliminary work of amending the Tridentine typical editions in harmony with the classical form of the Roman Rite before they are presented to local Churches for adaptation.

16. A. Chupungco, *Liturgies of the Future: The Process and Methods of Inculturation* (New York, 1989) 3–8.

Adaptation. In *Liturgies of the Future* I treated to a degree the terms "adaptation," "acculturation," and "inculturation" and the subject of the process and methods of inculturation.[17] It would be helpful nonetheless to cover again briefly the ground of what these terms mean in liturgical usage and to append the results of recent thinking on the subject. It would likewise be helpful to discuss at greater length the questions regarding the process and methods of liturgical inculturation.

"Adaptation" is the official word used by the Constitution on the Liturgy, especially in articles 37–40. This conciliar document uses *aptatio* and *accomodatio* synonymously, though in the chapter dealing with the sacraments and sacramentals *accomodatio* systematically replaces *aptatio*, seemingly as a via media, or measure of compromise. It will be remembered that at some point during the council discussion, *aptatio* began to sound menacing. Some of the council Fathers felt uncomfortable with the word, because at the height of the liturgical movement it came to be associated with the radical reform of the sacraments.

The distinction between *aptatio* and *accomodatio* began to take shape only with the publication of the typical editions of the conciliar liturgical books. The introductory part of these books normally contains two sections on adaptation: *De aptationibus*, which is the competence of the conference of bishops, and *De accomodationibus*, which is the right and duty of the minister. *Accomodatio* can be translated into English as "accommodation," but for obvious reason ICEL (International Commission on English in the Liturgy) chose to translate it as "adaptation." The distinction between the two Latin words, however, should not be lost. One type of adaptation pertains to the conference of bishops, which in this connection normally operates through the liturgical commission. The other type refers to what the minister can or should change in the celebration for pastoral reasons. The liturgical books give specific instances apropos of one and the other. The principal difference between *aptatio* and *accomodatio* is that the former, when approved by the Roman authority, requires that the changes be inserted in the ritual of the local Church, while the latter is a temporary change or modification of the rite made by

17. Ibid, 23–25; also see idem, *Cultural Adaptation of the Liturgy*, 42–57.

the minister to accommodate the special interest or needs of various groups.

What meaning does the Constitution on the Liturgy give to "adaptation?" SC 1 states that one of the aims of the council is "to adapt more suitably to the needs of our times those institutions that are subject to change." Taking its lead, we may assume that "adaptation" refers to the general program of Church renewal or updating. We have every reason to think that the Constitution on the Liturgy uses the term *aptatio* (or *accomodatio*) as an equivalent of the celebrated *aggiornamento* for which Pope John XXIII convoked Vatican II. To bring about the *aggiornamento*, or updating of the liturgy, it is unavoidable to adapt it to contemporary circumstances, to make the necessary adjustments, and to accommodate the current thinking on public worship. The Constitution on the Liturgy proposes two ways to achieve this: revision of the existing rites and adaptation to the needs of the time.

But "adaptation" is not an anthropological term; in fact, it is culturally neutral. That is why, when SC 37–40 addresses the question of adaptation to culture, it speaks of "Norms for Adapting the Liturgy to the Culture and Traditions of Various Peoples," which is referred to for short as "cultural adaptation." Furthermore, as G. Arbuckle has strongly pointed out, the term is associated with the manipulation of culture in the past on the part of colonizers. He therefore suggests that it be dropped from theological and liturgical vocabulary and replaced with a new and better term, namely "inculturation," which was coined to express "the evangelical implications of local church theology."[18]

"Inculturation" is now a familiar word in liturgical circles. But in deference to the established terminology of the Constitution on the Liturgy, official liturgical books continue to use the term "adaptation." This probably explains why the meaning of "adaptation" remains fluid and its use flexible. A good number of liturgists interchange the terms "adaptation" and "inculturation" or else combine them to form the hybrid expression "cultural adaptation." Those who do not wish to part from the conciliar usage argue that the term "inculturation"

18. G. Arbuckle, "Inculturation, Not Adaptation: Time to Change Terminology," *Worship* 60/6 (1986) 512–520.

has a number of rough edges that still need to be polished before it is released as a worthy substitute for "adaptation." Finally, those who opt to keep both terms recognize the value and use of each. They both refer to the updating of Church institutions. "Adaptation" denotes the general program of updating, while "inculturation" is one of the ways to achieve it.[19]

Inculturation. According to G. De Napoli, the term "inculturation" was coined in 1973 by G. L. Barney, a Protestant missionary who was professor at Nyack Alliance School of Theology in Nyack, New York. Stressing the need to keep the Christian message intact throughout the course of cultural exchange, Barney used the term in the context of frontier missions. He dutifully reminded his fellow missionaries that in the process of inculturating the supracultural components of the gospel into a new culture, their essential nature should neither be lost nor distorted.[20] Though Barney was apparently more concerned with the question of keeping the faith intact than with the coining of a technical term, he unknowingly enriched the Church vocabulary with a new word that quickly found favor with Church leaders and scholars.

The Jesuits did their share in launching the new term. The delegates to the 32nd General Congregation of the Society of Jesus, held in 1975, adopted the Latin *inculturatio* during their discussions.[21] The word was probably intended to be the Latin equivalent of "enculturation." Since Latin does not have the prefix "en," it became necessary

19. For instance, the Italian professors' congress in 1989 discussed the topic "Liturgy and Adaptation." The papers were published in *Liturgia e adattamento: Dimensioni culturali e teologico-pastorali* (Rome, 1990). Likewise, the Fourth International Liturgical Congress held by the Pontifical Liturgical Institute on May 6–10, 1991, carried the title "Cultural Adaptation of the Liturgy: Methods and Models."

20. G. Barney writes, "The essential nature of these supracultural components should neither be lost nor distorted but rather secured and interpreted clearly through the guidance of the Holy Spirit in 'inculturating' them into this new culture." "The Supracultural and the Cultural: Implications for Frontier Missions," *The Gospel and Frontier Peoples* (Pasadena, 1973). See G. De Napoli, "Inculturation as Communication," *Inculturation* 9 (1987) 71–98.

21. A. Crollius, "What Is So New About Inculturation?" *Gregorianum* 59 (1978) 721–738.

to use "in." The shift from "enculturation" to "inculturation" carried with it a change in the signification of words. A. Shorter points out that "enculturation" is in fact an anthropological jargon for "socialization," or the learning process "by which a person is inserted into his or her culture."[22] Quickly replacing "enculturation," "inculturation" ultimately took on a totally different meaning in theological, liturgical, and missiological circles.

In 1979 Pope John Paul II introduced "inculturation" into the official Church documents. In his address to the Pontifical Biblical Commission he observed that "the term 'acculturation' or 'inculturation' may be a neologism, but it expresses very well one of the elements of the great mystery of the incarnation."[23] In the course of that same year the pope elaborated on this statement in the apostolic exhortation *Catechesi tradendae*. After presenting the various conditions that should mark the relationship between catechesis and culture, he set out to explain that catechesis has an incarnational dimension. "Genuine catechists," he writes, "know that catechesis 'takes flesh' in the various cultures and milieux."[24] Through the mystery of the incarnation the Word of God took a human nature. Through the process of inculturation, catechesis, which is a form of proclaiming the gospel, acquires cultural expression.

In the seventies the liturgists took to the dissemination of information on the newly revised liturgical books. They were too busy with this immediate concern to worry about the question of how best to call adaptation. Among the first to use the term "inculturation" in connection with the liturgy was C. Valenziano, professor of cultural anthropology at the Pontifical Liturgical Institute in Rome. In an article on liturgy and popular religiosity, published in 1979, he names inculturation as a method that can bring about a mutual interaction between liturgy and the various forms of popular religiosity.[25]

What signification does "inculturation" convey when it is used in

22. A. Shorter, *Toward a Theology of Inculturation* (London, 1988) 5–6.

23. John Paul II, "Address to the Pontifical Biblical Commission," *Fede e cultura alla luce della Bibbia* (Turin, 1981) 5.

24. John Paul II, *Catechesi tradendae*, no. 53; GT, 667–668.

25. C. Valenziano, "La religiosità popolare in prospettiva antropologica," *Richerche sulla religiosità popolare* (Bologna, 1979) 83–110.

the field of liturgical study? To answer this question it is necessary to examine "inculturation" in relation to another term, namely "acculturation." For a while these two terms were employed interchangeably, but over the years it has become clearer that, though they are closely related, they are not exactly to be regarded as synonyms.

ACCULTURATION. In his enlightening work *Toward a Theology of Inculturation,* Shorter defines acculturation as "the encounter between one culture and another, or the encounter between two cultures." One important aspect of such an encounter, he explains, is that the communication between the two cultures comes about "on a footing of mutual respect and tolerance." But he adds that the encounter happens on an external basis. That is why "acculturation may lead merely to a juxtaposition of unassimilated cultural expressions, coming from various directions or origins." Nevertheless, encounter between two cultures is a process that starts with external contact. Sometimes this may result in a permanent state of juxtaposition of unrelated elements, but normally it should blossom into mutual assimilation. Shorter gives clear utterance to one of the basic principles of cultural anthropology when he affirms that "acculturation is a necessary condition of inculturation."[26]

Acculturation, which is a juxtaposition of two cultures, operates according to the dynamic of interaction. The two cultures interact "on a footing of mutual respect and tolerance." However, they do not go beyond the external forum or enter into the process of mutual assimilation. They do not affect each other's inner structure and organism. Acculturation may be described as the conjunction of three leading factors: juxtaposition, which is merely external; the dynamic of interaction; and the absence of mutual assimilation. We may compare acculturation to a chance uninvolved meeting of two strangers or to a casual hello and good-bye meeting of two persons. We may illustrate it with the formula $A+B = AB$. The two elements of this formula are merely placed side by side, so that neither undergoes any substantial or qualitative change. Thus they can withdraw any time from each other without any notable consequence.

26. Shorter, *Toward a Theology of Inculturation,* 6–8, 12; see Chupungco, *Liturgies of the Future,* 25–28.

In the liturgy a good example of acculturation took place during the baroque period. The official texts and rites of the liturgy, especially the Tridentine Mass, did not absorb the drama, festivity, and exuberance of the baroque culture. Because of rigid rubrical laws that barred the access of anything new, the baroque culture stayed at the periphery of the liturgy. The Tridentine liturgy, which was a direct descendant of medieval culture, also possessed particular elements of drama and ritual sensuousness. But by that time the Tridentine elements belonged to another age and people and no longer conformed with the contemporary expressions of culture.[27]

Juxtaposition continues to characterize some attempts to accommodate popular devotions. The practice of combining novenas or the Angelus with the Mass is a typical example of acculturation that stops at mere juxtaposition. The Mass and popular devotions often have nothing in common except that they are both prayers. An example that carries the official label of the Congregation for Divine Worship is the integration of a form of popular devotion, known as *encuentro*, with the Mass at Easter dawn. *Encuentro* consists of two processions, one with the image of the risen Christ and the other with a veiled image of the Blessed Virgin. They come from two directions and meet—hence, the name *encuentro*—at the town square, where the image of the Virgin is unveiled. Afterward, the procession proceeds to the church. In 1971 the Congregation for Divine Worship allowed the Philippine Church to replace the entrance rite of the Mass at Easter dawn with the *encuentro*. Here we have another example of juxtaposition. The texts of the Mass and this popular devotion possess nothing in common except that they both happen at dawn of Easter Sunday.

WHAT IS LITURGICAL INCULTURATION? Shorter defines "inculturation" as "the creative and dynamic relationship between the Christian message and a culture or cultures." He lists three of its notable traits. First, inculturation is an ongoing process and is relevant to every country or region where the faith has been sown. Second, Christian

27. See J. Jungmann, *The Mass of the Roman Rite* (Westminster, Md., 1986) 141–159 for the "The Mass in the Baroque Period"; idem, *Pastoral Liturgy* (London, 1962) 80–89 for the "Liturgical Life in the Baroque Period."

faith cannot exist except in a cultural form. And third, between Christian faith and culture there should be interaction and reciprocal assimilation.[28]

Apropos, it will be remembered that the extraordinary synod of bishops in 1985 touched on the question of inculturation. In the concluding declaration (no. D.4) the bishops sharply contrast inculturation with mere adaptation or acculturation: "Since the church is a communion, which is present throughout the world and joins diversity and unity, it takes up whatever it finds positive in all cultures. Inculturation, however, is different from a mere external adaptation, as it signifies an interior transformation of authentic cultural values through their integration into Christianity and the rooting of Christianity in various human cultures." The synod's definition contains the essential elements of inculturation, namely the process of reciprocal assimilation between Christianity and culture and the resulting interior transformation of culture on the one hand and the rooting of Christianity in culture on the other.

To the aforementioned elements of interaction and mutual assimilation we should add the dynamic of transculturation. In virtue of this dynamic the interacting parties are able to retain their identity or essential features throughout the process of mutual enrichment. Inculturation does not imperil the nature and values of Christianity as a revealed religion, nor does it jeopardize human culture as expression of society's life and aspirations. Christian worship should not end up being a mere ingredient of the local culture, nor should culture be reduced to an ancillary role. The process of interaction and mutual assimilation brings progress to both; it does not cause mutual extinction. What Pope John Paul II affirms about catechesis and culture has relevance to the point under discussion: "There would be no catechesis if it were the gospel that had to change when it came into contact with the cultures."[29] However, it is important to read also what is stated on the other side of the coin: there would be no true catechesis if the gospel were to destroy what is essential to a culture.

The difference between acculturation and inculturation may be illustrated with the formula $A+B = C$. Unlike the formula $A+B = AB$,

---

28. Shorter, *Toward a Theology of Inculturation*, 11.
29. John Paul II, *Catechesi tradendae*, no. 53; *GT*, 667.

this formula implies that the contact between *A* and *B* confers mutual enrichment on the interacting parties, so that *A* is no longer simply *A* but *C*, and likewise *B* is no longer simply *B* but *C*. However, because of the dynamic of transculturation, *A* does not become *B*, nor does *B* become *A*. Both undergo internal transformation, but in the process they do not lose their identity.

Liturgical inculturation, viewed from the side of the liturgy (the side of culture deserves a separate study), may be defined as the process of inserting the texts and rites of the liturgy into the framework of the local culture. As a result, the texts and rites assimilate the people's thought, language, value, ritual, symbolic, and artistic pattern.[30] Liturgical inculturation is basically the assimilation by the liturgy of local cultural patterns. It means that liturgy and culture share the same pattern of thinking, speaking, and expressing themselves through rites, symbols, and artistic forms. In short, the liturgy is inserted into the culture, history, and tradition of the people among whom the Church dwells. It begins to think, speak, and ritualize according to the local cultural pattern. If we settle for anything less than this, the liturgy of the local Church will remain at the periphery of our people's cultural experience. We cannot overstate the singular place of cultural pattern in the process of inculturation. It is where interaction and mutual assimilation between liturgy and culture normally take place.

No historical model typifies inculturation better than the classical Roman liturgy. This form of liturgy, which gained ascendancy in the Western world, flourished in Rome between the fifth and eighth centuries. It was authored by Gelasius, Vigilius, Leo the Great, and Gregory the Great; popes who belonged to the elite class of Roman

30. See Chupungco, *Liturgies of the Future*, 23–40; R. Gonzalez, "Adaptación, inculturación, creatividad: Planteamiento, problematica y perspectivas de profundización," *Phase* 158 (1987) 129–152; Vv.Aa, "L'inculturation," *La Maison-Dieu* 189 (1989); see also papers on liturgical inculturation read at the 1989 Societas Liturgica Meeting, *Studia liturgica* 20/1 (1990), especially P.-M. Gy, "The Inculturation of the Christian Liturgy in the West," 8–18; Amalorpavadass, "Theological Reflections on Inculturation," 36–54; Stauffer, "Inculturation and Church Architecture," 70–80; T. Berger, "The Women's Movement as a Liturgical Movement: A Form of Inculturation?" 55–64; A. Kavanagh, "Liturgical Inculturation: Looking to the Future," 70–80.

society, the group of the *homines classici* celebrated for their noble simplicity and sobriety, mastery of rhetorics, and practical sense. It is with such a group of people in mind that these popes developed that form of Roman liturgy for which history has reserved the designation of "classical." Its texts, even when translated into the modern languages, still betray the thought and language pattern of the people for whom they were composed.[31] In passing, it might be helpful to mention that during the classical period of the Roman liturgy inculturation was largely of a creative kind. We see this particularly in the representative sacramentaries of the period, such as the Old Gelasian, the Veronese, and the Gregorian. These contain prayer formulas that are original compositions.

In the eighth century another type of liturgical inculturation evolved in the Church of the Franco-Germanic empire. Unlike the Roman liturgy, which grew through the creative endeavor of popes, the Franco-Germanic liturgy developed primarily through contact with the classical shape of the Roman liturgy. The liturgists of the empire had to rework the texts and rites of the Roman books in order to accommodate the local people's temperament, which at that time was in diametric opposition to Roman sobriety. The result was a hybrid liturgy that kept the essential content of the Roman model, while investing it with a new and vigorous cultural form. The *Romano-Germanic Pontifical* of the tenth century, not to mention the so-called eccentric and exuberant types of sacramentaries dating from this period, surely infused charm, drama, and color into the habitually formal, austere, and reserved Roman liturgy.[32]

31. See E. Bishop, *Liturgica historica* (Oxford, 1962) 2–9, where the author describes "The Genius of the Roman Rite"; G. Dix, *The Shape of the Liturgy* (New York, 1982) 103–140, for the classical shape of the Eucharistic liturgy; Th. Klauser, *A Short History of the Western Liturgy* (Oxford, 1969) 59–68, for the classical traits of Roman euchology.

32. C. Vogel, "Les motifs de la romanisation du culte sous Pépin et Charlemagne," *Culto cristiano: Politica imperiale carolingia* (Todi, 1979) 17–20; E. Cattaneo, "L'età franco-carolingia," *Il culto cristiano in occidente* (Rome, 1984) 184–219; Klauser, *A Short History of the Western Liturgy,* 45–93.

Liturgical inculturation pertains ultimately to divine worship, to an activity that belongs to the realm of God's revelation and hence to an activity that defies any attempt at a systematic analysis. However, liturgical inculturation in itself is a branch of liturgical study. As such it has to be subjected to a system of thought; it has to be examined closely in the light of process and methodology.

Process is the course an activity takes, following well-defined steps or procedures. We are dealing here with what takes place between the *terminus a quo*, or point of departure, and the *terminus ad quem*, or point of arrival. The latter is the result of the process, the product of inculturation, while the former refers to the cultural entities that enter into the process of interaction. Since we are dealing with interaction, we should in reality speak of points of departure. The process itself may be pictured as lighting a candle at both ends. The idea is to make both ends meet in a literal, not idiomatic, sense. In the area of liturgy the process starts from two opposite points. These are the typical editions of Vatican II's liturgical books and the people's cultural pattern. The process of liturgical inculturation seeks to make them meet and interact, so that from their union a new *terminus ad quem*, a liturgy for the local Church, may be brought into existence. How this union can successfully be arrived at is a matter that pertains to methodology.

The Typical Editions of the Liturgical Books. Why the typical editions? Liturgical inculturation is a type of adaptation. Hence it works on existing liturgical texts and rites. On the whole, inculturation differs from creativity, which can dispense with existing Roman liturgical material. It is true that the classical Roman liturgy developed largely through creative endeavor. And we should not exclude the possibility that something similar could occur even today, especially in those local Churches where liturgical life is vibrant. However, after Vatican II, inculturation, for local Churches belonging to the Roman liturgical tradition or family, should normally start from existing models, and in practice the models are the typical editions of the liturgical books published by the Vatican after the council.

The mind of the Constitution on the Liturgy on the matter is clear:

the work of inculturation should be based on the typical editions of the liturgical books of Vatican II. The following conciliar texts support this.[33]

a. *SC* 38: "Provisions shall be made, even in the revision of liturgical books, for legitimate variations and adaptations to different groups, regions, and peoples, especially in mission lands."

b. *SC* 39: "Within the limits set by the typical editions of the liturgical books, it shall be for the competent, territorial ecclesiastical authority to specify adaptations, especially in the case of the administration of the sacraments, the sacramentals, processions, liturgical language, sacred music, and the arts."

c. *SC* 63b: "Particular rituals in harmony with the new edition of the Roman Ritual shall be prepared without delay by the competent, territorial ecclesiastical authority."

Given the complex nature of typical editions, it is evident that the process of liturgical inculturation does not use a shortcut. The principal elements of the typical editions need thorough examination. What is the historical background of the rite in question? What theology does its texts, rites, and symbols project? What pastoral and spiritual concerns does the rite embody? What possibilities for inculturation does it envisage? In the words of *SC* 23: "That sound tradition may be retained and yet the way remain open to legitimate progress, a careful investigation is always to be made into each part of the liturgy to be revised. This investigation should be theological, historical, and pastoral."

This is surely a tall order. But failure to comply could lead to liturgical and theological misfortunes. The following example will press the point. When infant confirmation became the normal practice after the sixth century, the kiss of peace, which the bishop gave previously to the confirmed adult, was for some reason revised to a light fatherly pat on the cheek of the child. By the thirteenth century in France and the Germanic region, the gesture evolved into a slap similar to what a man received when he was vested as a knight. In theological thinking confirmation began to be regarded as the sacrament

33. Chupungco, *Cultural Adaptation of the Liturgy,* 42–57.

that vested children with grace to do battle as soldiers of Christ. The passage from kiss to slap is one of the mishaps of inculturation, and the shift of emphasis from the Pentecostal outpouring of the Holy Spirit to a military sacrament is one of the tenacious misfortunes of sacramental theology.[34]

SC 23 speaks of "careful investigation." This involves exegesis of the original Latin text and research on the meaning of the gestures and symbols employed by the rite. The art of interpretation includes the science of semiotics, which examines the meaning, function, and relation to each other of the various persons and objects mentioned in liturgical texts and rubrical directions. Let us consider the following rubric: "When the people are assembled, the priest and the ministers proceed to the altar, while the entrance song is chanted." If this rubric, which says more than meets the eye, is to be subjected to the process of inculturation, it is necessary to examine the three things to which it directs the reader's attention. They are the coming together of the people, the action of the priest and ministers, and the entrance song. Not until these are placed under semiotic scrutiny as to their why, when, how, and where, can they enter into the process of inculturation.[35]

Exegesis has undeniably a major role in the translation and inculturation of Latin euchological texts. The Christmas collect *Deus, qui humanae substantiae dignitatem,* which may be regarded as one of the finest formularies to adorn the Roman Missal, was composed by Pope Leo the Great against the Manicheans, who viewed human nature as a depravation. Against this view, the Leonine text extols human nature and claims that it possesses a dignity created and redeemed by God himself. The mystery of the incarnation is a proof of this. Christ did not hesitate to share our human nature.[36] For some

34. A. Nocent, "La tradizione e la confermazione nella Chiesa latina dal X secolo fino a prima del Vaticano II," Anamnesis 3/1 (Genoa, 1986) 111. The thirteenth-century *Pontifical of Durand* carries the rubric "Et deinde [episcopus] dat sibi [ei] leviter alapam super genam, dicens: Pax tecum." *Le Pontifical Romain au Moyen-âge* 3, ed. M. Andrieu (Vatican City, 1973) bk. 1, 4, p. 334.

35. See A. Terrin, *Leitourgia* (Brescia, 1988). The volume is a useful exposition of what liturgical semiotics means and how it can be applied to the Roman order of Mass.

36. See A. Echiegu's exegesis of this collect, *Translating the Collects of the*

reason this exegetical aspect is ignored by the 1973 ICEL translation, which refers to human nature as "weakness." From the perspective of kenotic theology the ICEL text is surely nothing more than a faithful echo of the Pauline doctrine: Christ "emptied himself, taking the form of a servant" (Phil 2:7). But from an exegetical point of view it unwittingly and ironically falls into the Manichean snare.

Careful investigation requires exegesis not only of the liturgical texts but also of the conciliar and postconciliar documents on the liturgy. Its aim is to read the mind of the lawgiver, to give explicit utterance to those provisions that are stated by the document only in an implicit manner. A classic example is the one terse sentence that *SC* 72 devotes to the sacrament of penance: "The rites and formularies for the sacrament of penance are to be revised so that they more clearly express both the nature and effect of the sacrament." Through the art of hermeneutics we are able to discover the council's thinking on the subject, which is by no means evident from the text. By "nature" of the sacrament the council actually meant the social and ecclesial character of penance, and by "effect" the ancient practice of the laying on of hands, which it intended to restore in order to signify reconciliation.[37]

The Cultural Pattern. Along with the typical editions the cultural pattern of a people has a principal role to play in the process of liturgical inculturation. Cultural pattern is the typical mode of thinking, speaking, and expressing oneself through rites, symbols, and art forms. It affects society's values and ideology, social and family traditions, socioeconomic life, and political system. Cultural pattern cuts across everything that constitutes the life of a society. It is a people's prescribed system of reflecting on, verbalizing, and ritualizing the values, traditions, and experiences of life.

Cultural pattern is an innate quality of every sociocultural group

"Sollemnitates Domini" *of the* "Missale Romanum" *of Paul VI in the Language of the African* (Münster, 1984) 123–227. On the basis of his research the author proposes a dynamic translation of this collect into the Igbo language. See pp. 306–317 of his work.

37. Chupungco, *Liturgies of the Future,* 113–115. See F. Brambilla, "Ermeneutica teologica dell'adattamento liturgico," *Liturgia e adattamento: Dimensioni culturali e teologico-pastorali,* 39–83.

and is normally shared by the members born into the group. A person belongs to a particular society because he or she shares by birth the same cultural pattern. A society can be distinguished from another on the basis of differences in cultural pattern. However, different societies can share in common cross-cultural traits. That is why we can speak in a generic way of European, African, Latin American, Asian, and South Pacific cultural patterns, although each member of these major sociocultural groupings possesses a particular cultural pattern.

Cultural pattern can play a decisive role in liturgical change. When a local Church is vividly conscious of its cultural pattern, it will react negatively to a liturgy that employs a foreign cultural pattern. Thus, when the classical Roman liturgy migrated to the Franco-Germanic world, the local liturgists did exactly what they were expected to do. They revised the Roman liturgy to suit their colorful and vibrant culture. When the Romanized Franco-Germanic liturgy was introduced into the Eternal City, the Roman liturgists predictably tried to restore the liturgy to its original *sobrietas romana*.[38] The point is that a liturgy whose cultural pattern differs radically from that of the local Church has to adapt or be pushed to irrelevance.

In a sense it is easier to define cultural patterns than culture itself. And in the final analysis what matters is not whether we can define the nature and components of a particular culture but whether we are able to identify the principal elements that make up the cultural pattern. Scholars might be able to offer an accurate definition of the Roman culture during the classical period, but what we need to know when dealing with liturgical inculturation is the definition not of the Roman culture as such but of the cultural pattern of the Roman people. Liturgical research made a positive contribution when it identified the elements of sobriety, directness, brevity, simplicity, and practical sense as the constitutive ingredients of the Roman cultural pattern.[39]

38. The twelfth-century *Roman Pontifical* was a simplified form of the *Romano-Germanic Pontifical* of the tenth century, which in turn is a Gallicanized collection of earlier Roman material. See C. Vogel, *Medieval Liturgy: An Introduction to the Sources* (Washington, 1986) 230–252.

39. Bishop, *Liturgica historica*, 2–9; Klauser, *A Short History of the Western Liturgy*, 59–68.

A question that distresses liturgists in multicultural countries when the subject of inculturation is raised is how to define the culture of their own people. Is there, in the first place, one culture for the entire United States of America? If there were, it would be so multi-faceted and subject to constant change that it would at any rate elude definition. But inculturation does not need this kind of endeavor. Defining the culture of a people is often nothing more than an exercise in futility. What will definitely serve inculturation is a study that will determine the typical way a particular group of people, in the concrete circumstances of life, collectively thinks, speaks, and expresses itself through rites, symbols, and art forms. An inculturated liturgy is one whose shape, language, rites, symbols, and artistic expressions reflect the cultural pattern of the local Church.

THE METHODS OF INCULTURATION

The object of liturgical inculturation is to graft liturgical texts and rites onto the cultural pattern of the local Church. The question is which methods are available to us. If we examine historical and contemporary models of inculturation, we reach the conclusion that in the course of time several methods have been successfully employed. Three of these are dynamic equivalence, creative assimilation, and organic progression.

The effectiveness of these methods depends on several factors. The prevailing theological reflection at any given period on doctrinal and pastoral issues can affect the choice and application of the method. This is particularly apposite in regard to the method of organic progression. Another determining factor is the presence in a local Church of a culture that pulsates with life and vigor. Its own dynamism will normally flow into the Church's liturgy. In situations such as this the methods of creative assimilation and dynamic equivalence have been proven to be quite useful. Lastly, the pastoral needs of the worshiping community will prescribe the most appropriate method to be employed.

The Method of Dynamic Equivalence. Dynamic equivalence consists in replacing an element of the Roman liturgy with something in the local culture that has an equal meaning or value. By applying this method the linguistic, ritual, and symbolic elements of the Roman liturgy are reexpressed following a particular pattern of thought, speech, and ritual. The result is a liturgy whose language, rites, and symbols admirably relate to the community of worship as they evoke experiences of life, human values, and traditions, paint vivid images of God's creation, and call to mind the people's history.[40] A thing to remember about the method of dynamic equivalence is its dependence on the typical edition of the liturgical books. It can produce a creative liturgy, but not from pure imagination. It needs the official books as a basis.

The opposite of dynamic equivalence is the stationary or static. This consists in giving the equivalent of a word or a phrase without due reference to the people's cultural pattern, history, and experiences of life. The liturgy in probably every living language is replete with static equivalents. Examples abound: "mystery" for *mysterion*, "sacrament" for *sacramentum*, "dignity" for *dignitas*, "in memory of" for *anamnesis*, "come upon" for *epiclesis*. This manner of giving equivalents is of course a commendable measure to safeguard the doctrine of faith. It nips in the bud the risk of a translator becoming a traitor. But does it help the assembly's comprehension of what the liturgy is trying to communicate?

A couple of examples can elucidate the meaning of dynamic equivalence. It has been affirmed that the two basic terms in liturgy, namely "anamnesis" and "epiclesis," are also the two most intricate questions vexing liturgical inculturation. Recent theological reflection has sought to define these terms with accuracy and precision. In the process it has made them so technical that now they defy translation.

"Anamnesis" is commonly defined as the ritual memorial of Christ's paschal mystery. In virtue of this ritual memorial the paschal mystery becomes present in the worshiping assembly.[41] To express the concept of anamnesis, Latin employs the august and solemn words *memores* in the first three Eucharistic Prayers and *memoriale celebrantes* in the fourth. The 1973 ICEL translation of the *Roman Missal* uses respectively the phrases "celebrate the memory," "in memory of," "call to mind," and "celebrate the memorial." These are probably

40. Chupungco, *Liturgies of the Future*, 35–40.
41. S. Marsili, "Verso una teologia della liturgia," Anamnesis 1 (Turin, 1974) 47–84.

the nearest words to the profound concept of anamnesis in Latin and English. One thing is certain: like so many other liturgical terms, they need to be explained in reference to the technical term "anamnesis" in order to bring out their hidden theological insight. But is it enough to explain them? Should we not look for other expressions that can convey the meaning of anamnesis while they allude to the cultural experience of the worshiping assembly?

The proposed *Misa ng Bayang Pilipino* (Mass of the Filipino People), submitted to Rome by the conference of bishops in 1976, has made a significant effort to find a dynamic equivalent for anamnesis.[42] At the Eucharistic Prayer the narration of the Last Supper is prefaced with the Tagalog phrase *tandang-tanda pa namin,* literally, "how clearly we remember." The phrase indicates collective memory and is used to begin the narration of a historical event. It is the narrators' way of claiming that they were present when the event happened, that they witnessed it in person. That is why they can recount it vividly and to the last detail. Is this not perhaps what the Church wishes to say at the narration of the Last Supper? The Church was there, remembers clearly what took place that evening as Jesus sat at table with his disciples, and now faithfully transmits the experience from generation to generation.

The other concept is "epiclesis," which may be defined as the prayer of the Church invoking the presence of the Holy Spirit. It asks the Father to send the Holy Spirit on the sacramental elements and on the people, who receive the sacraments in order that the Holy Spirit may consecrate them to God and make them holy.[43] In the second Eucharistic Prayer ICEL expresses epiclesis with the phrase "let your Spirit come upon these gifts." ICEL's translation takes a step ahead of the Latin, which, with typical aversion for picturesque language, does not present the Holy Spirit as either coming or being sent. In fairness to the Latin text, however, we should note that the second Eucharistic Prayer, unlike the others, employs the imagery of *ros* (dew) which associates the Holy Spirit with the fecundating quality of water. The reference seems to be Isaiah 44:3. Likewise, the formulary for the blessing of baptismal water uses the verb *descendat.*

42. Text in Tagalog and English in Chupungco, *Towards a Filipino Liturgy,* 96–118.
43. A. Verheul, *Introduction to the Liturgy* (Hertfordshire, 1972) 51–72.

The *Misa ng Bayang Pilipino* has a graphic expression for epiclesis: *lukuban ng Espiritu Santo*, literally, "may the Holy Spirit take under his wings." The Tagalog verb *lukuban* means "to protect, to gather under the wings, or to brood." Used for epiclesis, it calls to mind the action of the bird brooding its eggs, thereby conveying the transforming and vivifying action of the Holy Spirit on the Eucharistic elements and the assembly. The Tagalog version of epiclesis makes us think of G. M. Hopkin's verse: "Because the Holy Ghost over the bent / World broods with warm breast and with ah! bright wings."

Along with imaginative language, idiomatic expressions are a rich mine of dynamic equivalence. The use of idiom, which is a type of living language peculiar to a people, is a convincing proof that the liturgy has assimilated the thought and language pattern of the worshiping community. The following example illustrates how idiomatic expressions can be employed in the liturgy as dynamic equivalents.

The Latin word *dignitas* is ordinarily translated into English as "dignity." Though "dignity" is a static equivalent, it is an accurate rendering of the Latin word. After all, English speakers give to the word "dignity" the same meaning the Romans gave to *dignitas*. However, inculturation is markedly partial to the method of dynamic equivalence. Along this line, A. Echiegu proposes an Igbo translation of the Christmas collect *Deus, qui humanae substantiae dignitatem*, using the method of dynamic equivalence. Although Igbo, the language of Nigeria, has an equivalent word for "dignity," the proposed translation has preferred to use the colorful idiomatic expression "to wear an eagle's feather." The feather of an eagle affixed to the hair indicates the dignity and position a person holds in society. Instead of merely affirming that God created the dignity of the human race, the proposed Igbo prayer praises God who gifts every man and woman he creates with the feather of an eagle.[44]

As regards the ritual elements, experience shows that inculturation using the method of dynamic equivalence is less cumbersome and can produce significant results. This is particularly true with gestures possessing strong symbolic value. In the liturgy everything can, of course, become a symbol. Every time we stand, sit, kneel, walk, raise our hands, bow our head, or turn toward the reader, we perform a li-

44. Echiegu, *Translating the Collects of the* "Sollemnitates Domini," 313.

turgical symbol. But there are gestures that eloquently convey the message to the assembly because of the symbolism they carry. The method of dynamic equivalence can be very useful for bestowing on ordinary liturgical gestures a more vivid cultural significance.

In the Zairean order of Mass the sign of peace takes place after the penitential rite, which concludes the Liturgy of the Word. In Zairean parishes the gesture consists in a simple handshake. However, the introduction to the Zairean order of Mass mentions an alternative form, which consists in washing hands in the same bowl of water as a symbol of purification, unity, and reconciliation. It is a graphic and expressive declaration of forgiveness, a concrete way of saying, "I wash away anything I have against you."[45] The introduction of alternative forms with pronounced cultural value such as this solves the difficulty arising from a handshake or a mere nod of greeting. In some cultural milieux the handshake is primarily a congratulatory sign, while a nod—even with a smile—can be quite formal and contrived, especially in societies that require people to be properly introduced to each other.

Another example of ritual dynamic equivalence is found in the rite of Communion in the *Misa ng Bayang Pilipino*. The rubric directs the priest to take Communion after the assembly and the other ministers. It is intended to express the Filipino concept and value of leadership and solicitude. To eat last is not only a sign of urbanity and social grace. Above all it represents service. Thus the host eats after the guests, because the host is expected to serve and move around. Parents take their meal after the children out of solicitude. At home a person forfeits or at least weakens his or her role as leader by taking food ahead of the others. In short, taking Communion last is, in the Filipino cultural context, an affirmation of the role of the priest as the president of the assembly.

The liturgy has replaceable elements, but not everything may be replaced. In order to know what may be changed and what must stay, it is important to make a distinction, insofar as this is possible, between the theological content and the liturgical form of a rite. Though this question has already been treated in the previous work

45. Text in Conférence Épiscopale du Zaïre, *Rite zaïrois de la célébration eucharistique* (Kinshasa, 1985) 44–45.

Liturgies of the Future, it would be useful to again briefly cover its chief points.[46]

The theological content is the meaning of the liturgical text or rite. Basically it is the paschal mystery present in various degrees and under different aspects in the celebration. At Mass the focus is on Christ's sacrifice on the cross; at baptism, on his burial and resurrection; at confirmation, on his act of sending the Holy Spirit on the day of Pentecost. Every liturgical rite contains, signifies, and celebrates the paschal mystery. However, this same mystery is expressed in different outward forms according to the meaning and purpose of each liturgical rite.

The liturgical form, which consists of ritual acts and formularies, gives visible expression to the theological content. Examples are the recitation of the Eucharistic Prayer over bread and wine, the washing with water while the Trinitarian formula is pronounced, the anointing with chrism, and the laying on of hands. Through the liturgical form the theological content of the sacraments receives outward, visible shape.

With this distinction in mind we need to observe a rather rigid principle. If the theological content or the liturgical form is of divine institution, it may not be replaced with another content or form that will modify the meaning originally intended by Christ. Thus, the washing with water and the Trinitarian formula are the irreplaceable liturgical form of baptism, and food and drink in memory of Christ's sacrifice are the irreplaceable elements of the Eucharist. However, the manner of washing and of expressing the Trinitarian formula, provided the theological content of baptism is kept, is within the realm of dynamic equivalence. The history of baptism witnesses to the plurality of ways to do the washing and to express the Trinitarian formula.

The distinction between theological content and liturgical form has practical implications for the liturgy of the Mass as well. Since the subject has been amply treated in *Liturgies of the Future*, a brief summary of the chief points will suffice.[47] The theological content of the Mass is the sacrifice of Christ on the cross, while its liturgical form is

46. Chupungco, *Liturgies of the Future*, 35–40, 71–82 for the order of Mass; 125–131 for Christian initiation; 163–172 for the liturgical year.
47. Ibid., 125–131.

the ritual meal consisting of the Liturgy of the Word and the Liturgy of the Eucharist. The Liturgy of the Word has a dialogical plan: God speaks (proclamation of the word of God), the priest explains the word (homily), and the people respond in prayer (general intercessions). In contrast, the Liturgy of the Eucharist imitates the shape of the Last Supper: the presentation of the gifts, the Eucharistic Prayer, and Communion evoke what Christ did at the Last Supper when he took the bread and the cup, said the prayer of blessing, and gave the broken bread and the cup to his disciples. Dialogue and ritual meal are the two anthropological realities that make up the liturgical form of the Mass and open the door to the method of dynamic equivalence. Every culture has its way of holding dialogues and celebrating a ritual meal.

The Eucharistic Prayer, since it is the high point of the entire celebration, deserves special attention. It is the prayer that directly and effectively invokes the presence of both sacrifice and meal. No other Mass formulary skillfully blends the idea of meal with sacrifice, the formula of table blessing with the act of oblation, and the narration of the Last Supper with the memorial of Christ's death on the cross. The Eucharistic Prayer is both formula of blessing and memorial of sacrifice, but its language has not always given them equal stress. In fact, the Roman Canon, whose language is preponderantly sacrificial, is called *actio sacrificii* by the sixth-century *Liber Pontificalis* in its notice on Pope Leo the Great. The following phrases confirm this observation: *accepta habeas; haec dona, haec munera, haec sancta sacrificia illibata; hanc igitur oblationem; quam oblationem . . . benedictam, adscriptam, ratam, rationabilem, acceptabilemque facere; hostiam puram, hostiam sanctam, hostiam immaculatam;* and *ex hac altaris participatione.*[48]

The other three Eucharistic Prayers, however, especially the one based on Hippolytus' *Apostolic Tradition,* use a type of language that refers markedly to the blessing said at a meal. A. Nocent writes that these prayers appear to be closer in structure and language to "the prayer of blessing which Christ certainly used at the last supper."

48. *Liber pontificalis,* vol. 2, ed. U. Prerovsky (Rome, 1978) 47, no. 5, p. 109. See M. Witczak, *The Language of Eucharistic Sacrifice:* Immolare *and* Immolatio *in Prefaces of the Roman Tradition* (Rome, 1987); A. Nocent, "La preghiera eucaristica del canone romano," Anamnesis 3/1 (Casale Monferrato, 1983) 229–245.

They may be regarded as formularies of table blessing that recall the paschal mystery through anamnesis.[49]

It is true that sacrificial words like *offerimus, hostia,* and *oblatio* are present in the new Eucharistic Prayers as well. We should note, however, that they are inserted in the framework of formularies for blessings said at meals. In other words, from the outset these prayers were conceived and composed as formularies for the Eucharistic table blessing more than for a sacrificial offering. This in no way confirms the allegations of critics that the new Eucharistic Prayers have eliminated from the Mass the doctrine of sacrifice. The accusation stems from the lack of clear distinction between the content of these new Eucharistic Prayers, which is Christ's definitive sacrifice on the cross, and their structural and linguistic form, which refers to his Last Supper.

Thus, the *Roman Missal* of Paul VI presents two models for the Eucharistic Prayer: one that is sacrificial in both content and form, and another whose content is sacrificial but whose form is patterned on table blessing. Evidently the orientation of each of the two models should be considered doctrinally sound, unless one intends to put the Holy See to task. But what interests us here is the choice of model for the composition of other Eucharistic Prayers. If we accept the distinction between content and form, then the question of which model to choose becomes moot and academic.

Thus, distinction, which here does not imply any physical separation, between theological content and liturgical form is a necessary condition for the correct application of the method of dynamic equivalence. One cannot overstate the principle enunciated by *SC* 21: "The liturgy is made up of immutable elements, divinely instituted, and of elements subject to change." Failure to make such a distinction could lead to confusion not only between theological content and liturgical form but also between what may not be changed and what can or needs to be changed.

The Method of Creative Assimilation. During the age of patristic creativity liturgical inculturation evolved through the assimilation of pertinent rites and linguistic expressions, religious or otherwise, used by contemporary society. In this way Church writers like Tertullian, Hip-

49. A. Nocent, "Le nuove preghiere eucaristiche," Anamnesis 3/1, pp. 247–257.

polytus, and Ambrose contributed to the progress of the shape of the rites of initiation. Classic examples are the baptismal anointing, the giving of the cup of milk and honey, and the washing of the feet of neophytes. Technical terms like *eiuratio* for baptismal renunciation, *fidei testatio* for profession of faith, *mystagogía*, and *initiatio* were entered, often for good, into the liturgical vocabulary.[50]

Pertinent rites borrowed from the socioreligious traditions of the period acquired a Christian meaning through the system of biblical typology. They often served as explanatory rites of the sacraments by elaborating on the core of the liturgical rite. Thus the rite of initiation evolved from the simple apostolic "washing in water with the word" (Eph 5:26) to a full liturgical celebration that included a prebaptismal anointing, the act of renunciation (toward the west) and profession of faith (toward the east), the blessing of baptismal water, and the postbaptismal rites of anointing with chrism, clothing with a white garment, and giving the lighted candle.[51]

This method played a significant part in the formation of the liturgy during the patristic period. However, in view of the provision of SC 38–39 and 63b concerning the typical editions, creative assimilation should not be regarded as the ordinary method of liturgical inculturation. According to these conciliar texts, the process of inculturation normally starts from the typical editions. In a sense the work of inculturation is more akin to translation than to creativity.

Apropos, we may read the concluding paragraph of the Instruction on the translation of liturgical texts with the methods of creative assimilation and dynamic equivalence in mind: "Texts translated from another language are clearly not sufficient for the celebration of a fully renewed liturgy. The creation of new texts will be necessary. But translation of texts transmitted through the tradition of the Church is the best school and discipline for the creation of new texts so that any new forms adopted should in some way grow organically from

50. Gy, "The Inculturation of the Christian Liturgy in the West," 8–18. Gy discusses the terms *confessio, absolutio,* and *paenitentia*; also see Chupungco, *Cultural Adaptation of the Liturgy,* 10–27.
51. B. Neunheuser, *Baptism and Confirmation* (New York, 1964); A. Kavanagh: *The Shape of Baptism: The Rite of Christian Initiation* (New York, 1978) 35–78; A. Nocent, "Preistoria e primi sviluppi dell'iniziazione (I–IV sec.)," Anamnesis 3/1 (Genoa, 1986) 17–39.

forms already in existence."[52] There will surely be occasions when a local Church's fully renewed liturgy will require inculturation through the application of creative assimilation. But inculturation based on the typical editions is the best school and discipline for creativity in the liturgy.

Creative assimilation is sometimes the only realistic method on hand to develop the shape of a local Church's particular ritual. This is clearly the case with the provision of SC 77, allowing the conferences of bishops "to draw up, in accord with art. 63, their own rite [of marriage], suited to the usages of place and people." Local Churches can considerably enrich the typical edition of the rite of marriage by expanding its ritual shape. In this connection it would be useful to look into the possibility of incorporating into the particular ritual suitable rites and symbols used in native marriage rites. Through creative assimilation the local Church's rite of marriage will acquire a new shape, possibly a new plan and a new set of formularies, and explanatory rites.[53] The new features will not serve as dynamic equivalents of the elements present in the typical edition. They will act the part of protagonists in the elaboration of a new rite. We recall that during the early centuries the Greco-Roman rites of initiation played a similar part in the development of the shape of baptism.

Creative assimilation may be employed with advantage for the inculturation of other liturgical celebrations like funerals and blessings and the introduction of new liturgical feasts inspired by historical events and local festivals of national significance. Particular attention should be given to the introductory and explanatory rites of sacramental celebrations. These rites can readily accommodate new features, because they do not exhaust all that can be said about the sacraments. There are surely other doctrinal points concerning baptism besides what chrism, the white garment, and the lighted candle represent. Baptism also produces such effects as membership in the

52. Consilium, Instruction *Comme le prévoit*, January 25, 1969, no. 43. English text in *Documents on the Liturgy, 1963–1979: Conciliar, Papal, and Curial Texts* (Collegeville, 1982) 291. Henceforth *DOL*.

53. R. Serrano, *Towards a Cultural Adaptation of the Rite of Marriage* (Rome, 1987). This published thesis was presented for doctorate to the Pontifical Liturgical Institute.

Christian community, participation in the Eucharist, and call to service. Depending on the local Church's doctrinal or moral priorities, suitable introductory and explanatory rites borrowed from culture can be introduced into the rite of baptism. These can eventually replace, if it is opportune to do so, some of the explanatory rites in the typical edition.

Along this line G. Ramshaw-Schmidt makes a timely suggestion in a proposed rite, "Celebrating Baptism in Stages."[54] After the giving of the lighted candle to each family of the newly baptized, "the children are welcomed to the table of the Eucharist" with words exhorting the families to receive the children at the Eucharistic table. The rite concludes with the presentation of the children to the community of the Church: "The presider may carry a child, or have the families carry their respective children, up and down the aisles and around the church, holding them high and showing the church its newest members."[55] These additional explanatory rites fall within the ambit of creative assimilation. In mission lands where native initiatory rites are still practiced, the new introductory and explanatory rites will have a more obvious cultural overtone. In this connection SC 65 makes the following provision: "With art. 37–40 of this Constitution as the norm, it is lawful in mission lands to allow, besides what is part of Christian tradition, those initiation elements in use among individual peoples, to the extent that such elements are compatible with the Christian rite of initiation."

The Method of Organic Progression. The third method of inculturation is what may be called "organic progression." It is the work of supplementing and completing the shape of the liturgy established by the Constitution on the Liturgy and by the Holy See after the council. In the light of the postconciliar experiences of local Churches, the typical editions of liturgical books are reread with the purpose of filling in what they lack or of completing what they only partially and imperfectly state. It is a way of saying that the new liturgical forms, which were not envisaged by the Constitution on the

54. G. Ramshaw-Schmidt, "Celebrating Baptism in Stages: A Proposal," *Alternative Futures for Worship*, 2:137–155.
55. Ibid., 152–153.

Liturgy or the typical editions, should have been there all along, that they would surely have been included in the liturgical rite had it been drawn up today. In short, the method is progressive because of the new shape it gives to the liturgy. At the same time it is organic because its result complies with the basic intention of the liturgical documents and, on a wider breadth, with the nature and tradition of the liturgy.[56]

SC 23 underlies the concept of organic progression: "Care must be taken that any new forms adopted should in some way grow organically from forms already existing." The conciliar commission explained that in the text the phrase "new forms" amply suggests the creation of new rites. The text closes no doors, though it instills the need for continuity and places the Church on guard against impertinent innovations.[57]

Organic progression moves onward from where the framers of the Constitution on the Liturgy or the revisors of the typical editions stopped. The method does not consist in a gradual unfolding of the liturgical shape from a simple to a complex form. It is known for a fact that the conciliar commission entrusted the decision on certain matters of importance to the postconciliar commission. Two examples are the proposal to create new liturgical feasts and the question of transferring, in particular circumstances, the weekly obligation from Sunday to another day of the week.[58] On other occasions the conciliar commission did not think it timely to enter into disputed theological questions like the repetition of anointing in the course of the same illness.[59] And to reach a consensus the commission sometimes settled for a compromise, or via media, of which SC 63a is a classic case: "Particular law remaining in force, the use of the Latin language is to be preserved in the Latin rites."

The foregoing observations argue the existence of lacunae in the Constitution on the Liturgy. Nowhere does it make provision for the

---

56. For a more extensive discussion of this subject see A. Chupungco, "Inculturation and the Organic Progression of the Liturgy," *Ecclesia orans* 7 (1990/1) 7–21.

57. *Schema Constitutionis de Sacra Liturgia*, ch. 1, *emendationes* 4 (Vatican City, 1967) 8. Henceforth *Schema*.

58. Ibid., *De anno liturgico, emendationes* (Vatican City, 1968) 11.

59. Ibid., *De ceteris sacramentis, modus* 3 (Vatican City, 1968) no. 60, p. 16.

adaptation of the order of Mass. *SC* 50 confines itself to the norms and criteria to be followed in revising the *Tridentine Missal*. The Constitution does not address the question of repeating the rite of anointing during the same illness, though such was the practice until the thirteenth century. Nor does it mention the possibility of using any kind of plant oil for the sacrament of the sick, though several bishops from the missions requested it. Why these lacunae? Regarding the issue of repeating the sacrament of anointing, the council Fathers clearly did not wish to enter into a disputed question. In fact, the proposed text of the Constitution did originally contain a provision reviving the practice, but the council voted to have it expunged. At the same time, the centuries-old tradition of keeping one order of Mass for the Roman Rite seems to have influenced the council Fathers to bar future adaptations from consideration. As regards the use of other plant oils for anointing the sick, it seems that the council simply overlooked its urgency.

There are also noticeable lacunae in the typical editions of the postconciliar liturgical books. Recognizing the textual and ritual poverty of the rite of marriage, *SC* 77 has ordained that it be revised and enriched. The rite was revised in 1969 and again in 1990, but there is a lingering consciousness that lacunae still remain. The 1990 revised typical edition continues to carry the provision that "the formularies of the Roman rite can be adapted, or as the case may be, supplemented (including the questions before the consent and the actual words of consent)."[60] The presence of lacunae in the typical edition shows that local Churches have a significant part to play in the process of organic progression. They alone possess a fuller estimation of their pastoral and cultural needs.

After the council several lacunae were filled during the reign of Pope Paul VI. The ferment of change profoundly affecting the Church could not be ignored by the Holy See. All over the world, especially in the missions, there was a clamor for new forms, some of which the Constitution on the Liturgy had not and could not have foreseen. As Pope Paul VI has counseled the revisors of the liturgical books, "the voice of the church today must not be so constricted that

60. *Ordo celebrandi matrimonium, editio typica altera* (Vatican City, 1991) no. 41, p. 9.

it could not sing a new song, should the inspiration of the Holy Spirit move it to do so."[61]

In the spirit of organic progression the postconciliar revisors promptly attended to the various lacunae in the conciliar document. The instances where organic progression has been clearly at work are many. The salient ones are the use of the vernacular in all liturgical celebrations; the incorporation into the typical editions of new elements like the general absolution and the new Eucharistic Prayers; the faculty to repeat anointing in the course of the same illness; the permission to use another kind of plant oil for the sacrament of the sick; and the possibility to draw up particular orders of Mass.

The work of organic progression should continue on the level of the local Churches. The typical editions normally offer a wide range of options and possibilities. But the breadth of inculturation should not be hemmed in by the provisions contained in a document. The typical editions cannot possibly envisage for a local Church all the options and possibilities of inculturation. Thus their provision will prove insufficient and at times also deficient when placed vis-à-vis the demand for a truly inculturated liturgy. Local Churches can look up to the Holy See not only to obtain the needed faculty or consent but also to learn from its happy and fruitful experience after the council how to deal with lacunae and the unfinished project of reform.

Since organic progression consists in supplying what was left unsaid in the liturgical documents, it is in a sense a continuation of the work of the council on the part of the Holy See or of the work of the Holy See on the part of the local Churches. Organic progression does not regard the present phase of liturgical reform as something so final or definitive that it leaves no space for further development. Considered in this light, the Constitution on the Liturgy, so long as another council does not produce a new one, will not become obsolete, because it was not completed in the first place. It merely ushered in the era of conciliar reform.

Organic progression occupies an important place in postconciliar reform. It serves as a justification or perhaps an apologetic of what has transpired in the area of the liturgy after Vatican II. Counter-

61. Paul VI, *Address to the Members and* Periti *of the Consilium,* October 13, 1966, in *DOL,* 224.

reformation groups have assailed time and again the liturgical reform executed by the Holy See on grounds of trespassing the limits set by the Constitution on the Liturgy.[62] But criticisms mixed with frustration and censure are even louder against the efforts of local Churches to inculturate the liturgy. We certainly do not even think of justifying blatant abuses by a recourse to organic progression. But we cannot close the door to progress simply because the text of the official documents does not stipulate anything explicit or implicit on the matter. There are lacunae and these have to be filled. The unfinished projects of conciliar reform have to be completed.

In conclusion we may state the conviction that if organic progression had not had a role in the postconciliar revision of the typical editions of the liturgical books, the Church today would have been sadly deprived of a richer liturgical life. Similarly, if organic progression does not influence the work of inculturation among local Churches, the liturgy for the local Church has little prospect of becoming a reality.

TOWARD LITURGICAL CREATIVITY

To complete the design of this chapter it is necessary to address the issue of liturgical creativity. Inculturation, which belongs to the category of dynamic translation, is not the final step in the process of bringing about the reality of the liturgy for a local Church. The 1969 Instruction on the translation of liturgical texts plainly affirms that "texts translated from another language are clearly not sufficient for the celebration of a fully renewed liturgy. The creation of new texts will be necessary."[63] Any form of inculturated liturgy, however culturally dynamic in its expression, remains a type of translation and hence cannot satisfy all the requirements for a liturgy that is able to answer every local need. At some point there will be a need to do more than just a dynamic translation of the Roman liturgy.

Liturgical creativity covers a wide spectrum of meaning ranging

62. A. Bugnini, *The Reform of the Liturgy, 1948–1975* (Collegeville, 1990), 277–301. Bugnini lists among the counterreformation groups the Una Voce, the Fraternity of St. Pius X founded by Archbishop M. Lefebvre, and the Catholic Traditionalist Movement.

63. Consilium, Instruction *Comme le prévoit*, no. 43; *DOL*, 291.

from absolutely new forms of liturgy to a simple case of adaptation. It is often associated with the imaginative or original shaping of liturgical rites, which are commonly known as "creative liturgies." These are often conceived for special celebrations, especially with young people, for the purpose of making the official worship more relevant or at least more palatable to the group.[64] It is regrettable that creative liturgies sometimes give the impression of being the product of mere fantasy and having only a vague reference, if at all, to the principles and traditions of the liturgy.

As the words "liturgical creativity" suggest, we are dealing here with liturgical rites formed independently of the provision, whether explicit or implicit, of the typical editions of the Roman books. Needless to say, such rites, if they are to be recognized by the Church as forms of official worship, must have some basis in or reference to liturgical tradition and must follow the principles concerning Christian worship. In the liturgy the concept of creativity is not of the absolute kind referred to by scholastic philosophers as *creatio ex nihilo sui et subiecti.* The liturgy is, in part, revealed and instituted by Christ, or as *SC* 21 puts it, "The liturgy is made up of immutable elements, divinely instituted, and of elements subject to change." These immutable elements have been transmitted by tradition, and they subsist in every new liturgical rite instituted by the Church. Liturgical creativity does not mean the total disregard for tradition or any preexisting liturgical material. It simply means that it is concerned with new liturgical forms not based on the Roman typical editions.

Culture, technology, and ideology influence the shape of creative liturgies. We observe this in such examples of creative ritualization as the symbolic dance at the offertory procession or during the chanting of the *Magnificat* at vespers, the mimetic interpretation of the gospel reading, and the use at the general intercessions of audiovisuals, also known in the seventies and the eighties as multimedia. In situations of sociopolitical discontent these forms can have ideological underpinnings. They can dramatize the people's sentiments of anger and frustration. That is why creative liturgies are sometimes associated with contextualization. Culture and ideology likewise affect creative texts. These are original compositions removed in theme and charac-

64. See B. Kenny, ed., *Children's Liturgies* (New York, 1977).

ter from the corpus of Roman formularies. In situations of malcontentedness they vent public grievances.

It would not be correct, however, to identify creative liturgies wholly with contextualization. Symbolic dance is an art form able to convey the spirit of joy, sorrow, or gratitude present in the liturgical rite. The mimetic interpretation of a biblical passage can have a catechetical value. Audiovisuals can engrave the message more deeply in the memory of the assembly.[65] Furthermore, there are rites, increasingly called "alternative liturgies," whose aim is to give expression to those facets of liturgical tradition or modern life that are not considered by the Roman rite.[66] Viewing infant baptism also in the light of modern human sciences or the sacrament of reconciliation according to its psychological dimensions is one of the suggested approaches to alternative liturgies.[67]

The concept of liturgical creativity can be applied in a broad sense to acculturated and inculturated liturgies. These too are products of creativity. Indeed, it is difficult to think of any example of inculturation where creative spirit and imaginative skill have not been at work. The fact alone that a new liturgical form based on the typical edition has been brought into existence through inculturation is already a clear proof that creativity has been part of the process. However, inculturated liturgy differs from other creative liturgies, because unlike these it is by definition related, even if only loosely, to the Roman typical editions.

The history of the liturgy attests to the Church's creative skill in shaping new rites in order to transmit the message in ways that could be understood and appreciated by the worshiping community. One of the ways favored by the council is the dynamic translation of the Roman liturgy, or inculturation, whereby the original content of the rite is preserved. But Christian life is richer in content and scope than the Roman liturgy. There is more to life than what the Roman formularies and rites are able to embody. In short, inculturation alone

65. K. Schneider and A. Ortegel, *Light Multimedia: Techniques for Celebration* (Chicago, 1982).
66. See *Alternative Futures for Worship*, 7 vols.
67. A. Thompson, "Infant Baptism in the Light of the Human Sciences," ibid., 2:55–102; P. Roy: "Psychological Dimensions of Reconciliation," ibid., 4:17–31.

cannot fully satisfy all the requirements for a truly renewed liturgy of a local Church. Creativity, which has always been an inherent feature of the Church's worship, is sometimes not a mere option but an imperative for a local Church that wants its liturgy to be relevant and have impact on the life of the faithful.

Chapter Two

Sacramentals and Liturgical Inculturation

A DEFINITION OF SACRAMENTALS

Sacramentals, or the "minor sacraments," as Hugh of St. Victor called them—for that is what they are in reality—tend to be regarded as adjuncts to the sacraments. This attitude unfortunately often gives the impression that sacramentals do not hold in the economy of salvation any place of significance. Nothing, however, is further from the truth. Although sacramentals, unlike the sacraments, are not of divine institution and do not produce their effect *ex opere operato*, it would be a serious mistake to cast on them a mere sideglance, or worse, bypass them altogether. The Church has always been keenly aware that the spiritual life of the faithful is not confined to participation in the sacraments and that sacramentals play a significant role in nurturing the effect of sacraments.

When we set the liturgy in the framework of the different cycles of human life and activities, we come to realize that not only the Eucharist and other sacraments, the Divine Office, and the liturgical year, but also the sacramentals occupy allotted places. While the Divine Office sanctifies the cycle of the day and the liturgical feasts consecrate the cycle of the year and seasons to the paschal mystery, the sacramentals complete, supplement, or extend the effect of sanctification brought about by the sacraments. Besides the ground of human life and activities covered by the seven sacraments, there is a myriad of other situations in the life of an individual, a family, or a community that are in need of the Church's prayer and God's blessing. Some of these, like religious profession, Christian funerals, the blessing of a new home, and the dedication of a church, are significant turning points in the lives of individuals and communities. In times like these the Church invokes God's presence and prays for special grace.

The Constitution on the Liturgy, article 60, copying in part the classical definition of sacramentals by the 1917 Code of Canon Law, explains their nature and purpose in these words: "The church has instituted sacramentals. These are sacred signs bearing a kind of resemblance to the sacraments: they signify effects, particularly of a spiritual kind, which are obtained through the church's intercession. They dispose people to receive the chief effect of the sacraments and they make holy various occasions in human life." The noted commentator on the Constitution on the Liturgy, J. Crichton, writes apropos of the conciliar definition of sacramentals: "No doubt to avoid a purely theological discussion (with which it is not concerned) the Constitution gives what is almost the definition of sacramentals of the Code of Canon Law (c.1144)."[1]

But there are notable differences. While the old Code defines sacramentals as objects (*res*) or actions (*actiones*), the Constitution on the Liturgy speaks of them as signs (*signa*). Since the Constitution uses the same word for the sacraments, it is reasonable to think that the stress on action or celebration given by the conciliar document to the sacraments should apply as well to the sacramentals. For sacramentals are *in genere signi*. More than being mere objects of devotion, they are liturgical activities or celebrations of the worshiping community. For this reason SC 79 directs that "the sacramentals are to be reviewed in the light of the primary criterion that the faithful participate intelligently, actively, and easily." In other words, sacramentals are above all liturgical celebrations. Certain objects are, of course, also called sacramentals inasmuch as they are destined for use in the celebration of worship. Examples of these are holy water, and candles, ashes, and palm branches blessed respectively on the feast of the Presentation of Our Lord, Ash Wednesday, and Palm Sunday. Medals and the rosary are less appropriately called sacramentals, since they have no part in the liturgy.

C. Vagaggini, who alone among liturgist-theologians has treated extensively the topic of sacramentals, distinguishes two types of sac-

---

1. J. Crichton, *The Church's Worship* (London, 1964) 164. Canon 1144 says: "Sacramentalia sunt res aut actiones quibus Ecclesia, in aliquam Sacramentorum imitationem, uti solet ad obtinendos ex sua impetratione effectus praesertim spirituales." The 1983 Code of Canon Law (can. 1166) borrowed its definition from SC 60.

ramentals, namely those that are things and those that are actions. He writes: "The sacramentals that are things are those which remain even after the action has taken place, such as holy water, blessed candles, blessed olive or palm branches, the ashes of Ash Wednesday. The sacramentals that are actions are those which pass with the action itself with which they have been constituted."[2] We can perceive a particular similarity between the objects used for the celebration of sacramentals and such elements as water and oil for the sacraments. In fact, by tradition we speak of baptismal water, chrism, oil of the catechumens, and oil for the sick as sacraments, although the sacrament itself consists properly of ritual action or celebration.

Another difference is that the council's definition attaches sacramentals more closely to the sacraments: they not only bear a resemblance to the sacraments, they also dispose people to receive the effect of the sacraments. The design to connect the sacramentals with the sacraments is evident in the way the Constitution banded them together in a single chapter. SC 61, 62, and 63 are introductory articles that deal with both. To a *modus* presented to the council suggesting that sacramentals be treated in a separate chapter the conciliar commission answered: "By their nature sacramentals are intimately joined to the sacraments, and it is the practice to deal with both under the same heading."[3]

A third difference is the explicit mention of the sanctifying power of the sacramentals: "They make holy various occasions in human life." After examining at great length this aspect of the sacramentals, Vagaggini concludes that "a sacramental, in today's restricted sense, consists immediately in a prayer of impetration by the Church and, by means of that prayer, in a sanctification."[4] SC 61 gives a succinct summation of this subject matter: "For well-disposed members of the faithful, the effect of the liturgy of the sacraments and sacramentals is that almost every event in their lives is made holy by divine grace

2. C. Vagaggini, *Theological Dimensions of the Liturgy* (Collegeville, 1976) 86; see also A. Donghi, "Sacramentales," *Nuevo diccionario de liturgia*, ed. D. Sartore and A. Triacca (Madrid, 1987) 1778–1797.

3. *Schema Constitutionis de Sacra Liturgia, modus 3*, (Vatican City, 1963) no. 27, p. 10. Henceforth *Schema*. The translations are mine.

4. Vagaggini, *Theological Dimensions of the Liturgy*, 88.

that flows from the paschal mystery of Christ's passion, death, and resurrection, the fount from which all sacraments and sacramentals draw their power. The liturgy means also that there is hardly any proper use of material things that cannot thus be directed toward human sanctification and the praise of God." Though they do not possess the same intensity and efficaciousness as the sacraments, sacramentals are means of human sanctification. Like the sacraments, they draw their power from the paschal mystery.

The Constitution on the Liturgy, which incidentally takes no notice of sacramentals as objects, gives only a limited list of sacramentals. SC 79 mentions blessings, SC 80 the rites for the consecration of virgins and of religious profession, SC 81 the rite of funerals, and SC 82 the rite for the burial of infants. After the council a good number of sacramentals were published in separate rituals, namely the blessing of abbots and abbesses, the consecration of virgins, religious profession, the institution of lectors and acolytes, the dedication of a church and an altar, the blessing of oils, the rite of funerals, and the rite of crowning images of the Blessed Virgin Mary. The *Book of Blessings*, published in 1984, confines itself to those blessings that do not have a separate ritual. These blessings, which number as many as forty-eight headings, deal with the blessing of persons, animals, and things including fields, buildings, instruments of work, vehicles, and devotional objects. Lastly, the *Caeremoniale Episcoporum*, published also in 1984, devotes a part of the book to those sacramentals that are normally celebrated by the bishop.[5]

THE CONCILIAR PRINCIPLES OF INCULTURATION

The vast material on sacramentals, which one writer has compared to a jungle, will not permit a thorough discussion of how each of the sacramentals can be inculturated. There are, however, general principles clearly enunciated by the Constitution on the Liturgy that define the nature and purpose of sacramentals and hence, short of being es-

5. *I sacramentali e le benedizioni,* Anamnesis 7 (Genoa, 1989), studies the major forms of sacramentals: consecration of virgins, blessing of abbots and abbesses, religious and monastic profession, dedication of a church and altar, blessings, exorcisms, and rite of funerals.

sential, are of utmost importance to the work of inculturation. Furthermore, the typical editions for the sacramentals published after the council offer various suggestions on how they can be adapted to the needs of local Churches. These suggestions have a practical bearing on the inculturation of the rites of different sacramentals.

The Constitution on the Liturgy devotes eight articles to sacramentals: *SC* 60–63 and 79–82. *SC* 60 and 61 define the nature and effect of sacramentals; *SC* 62, 63, and 79 state the principles that govern their reform; and the remaining articles lay down the specific norms for the revision of the rite for the consecration of virgins, the rite of religious profession, and the rite of funerals.

A closer examination of *SC* 60–63 and 79 will shed light on what the council had in mind when it issued the order to revise the liturgy of the sacramentals. "With the passage of time," *SC* 62 observes, "certain features have crept into the rites of the sacraments and sacramentals that have made their nature and purpose less clear to the people of today; hence some changes have become necessary as adaptations to the needs of our own times." The intention behind the conciliar decree concerning the revision and consequently the adaptation (or inculturation) of sacramentals becomes clearer if the decree is viewed from its theological, cultural, and pastoral underpinnings.

The Theological Principles. The sacramentals instituted by the Church "bear a kind of resemblance to the sacraments." Like the sacraments, they are sacred signs that are performed or celebrated as liturgical rites to signify effects, particularly of a spiritual kind. Vagaggini names the chief effects of sacramentals: first, actual grace for persons and by means of it the recovery or increase of sanctifying grace; second, the prevention of diabolical influence on persons or things; and third, temporal graces with a view to the spiritual good of the person.[6] However, unlike the sacraments, the sacramentals produce such effects through the intercessory prayer of the Church, or in traditional parlance, *ex opere operantis Ecclesiae.* This phrase, which is a little difficult to translate, means that when sacramentals are celebrated in the manner prescribed by the Church for their validity, the intercessory role of the Church is signified and realized. Be-

6. Vagaggini, *Theological Dimensions of the Liturgy*, 113.

cause of the Church's union with Christ, who is its head, God accepts the Church's prayer.[7] In other words, the value and efficacy of the prayer of the Church rest ultimately on Christ's own priestly prayer.

Like the sacraments, the sacramentals draw their power from the paschal mystery. We should not hesitate to claim that the liturgy of the sacramentals contains and proclaims the death and resurrection of Jesus. In the words of Vagaggini, "all sacramentals, in as much as they involve sanctification, are also signs commemorative of Christ's Passion as meritorious cause of this sanctification."[8] Like the sacraments, the sacramentals have been instituted for the purpose of making holy by the divine grace that flows from the same paschal mystery various occasions in the life of well-disposed members of the faithful. *SC* 61 teaches that in the liturgy "there is hardly any proper use of material things that cannot be directed toward human sanctification and the praise of God." Finally, in relation to the sacraments, the sacramentals dispose the faithful to receive the chief effect of the sacraments. They lead the faithful to the sacraments, they remind them of the effect and obligations flowing from the sacraments, and they extend in time and in various situations of life the experience of Christ's saving mysteries.[9] The nature and effects of sacramentals are so grafted on to the sacraments that it is difficult to speak of them in isolation.

These theological principles profoundly influence any project of inculturating the liturgy of sacramentals. In this connection, it is important to bear in mind that sacramentals hold a particular place in the scheme of the Church's sacramental life. This scheme includes the following basic points: first, sacramentals resemble the sacraments; second, they dispose the faithful to receive the chief effect of

7. See Vagaggini's explanation of the efficacy of liturgical signs instituted by the Church, ibid., 112–127.

8. Ibid., 90.

9. A *modus* presented during the council, which was not incorporated into the text because it was submitted too late, explains this point well: "Sed ut consecratio mundi a Verbo incarnato procedens et per Sacramenta in homines propagata latius in dies progrediatur atque fidelium vitam tam socialem quam individualem intimius penetret, Sancta Mater Ecclesia instituit sacra signa, quae dicuntur Sacramentalia." *Schema, modus* 3, no. 26, p. 10.

the sacraments; and third, they make holy various occasions in human life. These three points deserve closer examination.

First, since sacramentals resemble the sacraments, they share in some way the qualities inherent to the sacraments. Hence, SC 7's doctrine on the nature of the liturgy applies, though in lesser degree than in the case of the sacraments, to sacramentals: "Every liturgical celebration, because it is an action of Christ the Priest and of his Body which is the Church, is a sacred action surpassing all others; no other action of the Church can equal its effectiveness by the same title and to the same degree." Sacramentals are not considered sacraments, but they are nonetheless true liturgical celebrations, an exercise of the priestly office of Jesus Christ, an action of Christ the Priest and of the Church, which he associates with himself. Hence, they are sacred actions surpassing in effectiveness those that are not included in the category of liturgy.

Furthermore, since "Christ is always present in his Church, especially in its liturgical celebrations," it is evident that he is also present when sacramentals are celebrated. Though they are not instituted personally by Christ, they belong to the body of official worship attributed to his priestly office. Vagaggini's treatise on this doctrinal point is most enlightening. He explains that the sacramentals are "the prayer which the Church, or rather Christ, considers in all respects as His own, in which, so to speak, He considers Himself wholly engaged before God." That is why, continues Vagaggini, in the celebration of sacramentals "Christ as Head of His members assumes responsibility before God, so to speak, for the performance of the prayer and the rite which He by special mandate has given power to the hierarchy to institute and to perform in His name as Head of the Church."[10] We should add that in any event Christ is present in the word of God, which is proclaimed when sacramentals are celebrated. According to SC 7, "He is present in his word, since it is he himself who speaks when the holy Scriptures are read in the Church."

It is the accepted teaching today that the presence of Christ in every liturgical celebration is real, as opposed to something merely subjective and imaginary. In his celebrated encyclical *Mysterium fidei* Pope Paul VI clarified the issue when he wrote that the Eucharistic

10. Vagaggini, *Theological Dimensions of the Liturgy,* 116.

presence "is called the *real presence* not to exclude the other kinds as though they were not real, but because it is real par excellence, since it is substantial, in the sense that Christ whole and entire, God and man, becomes present."[11] The liturgist-theologian S. Marsili makes the following elucidation: "Between the eucharistic 'real presence' and the other 'real presences' *there is no difference* with regard to the 'presence' of Christ and the 'reality' of his presence. The difference lies in the *manner* in which these various 'presences' are made 'real.'"[12] In the case of the Eucharist, the manner of his presence is substantial, or in the words of Pope Paul VI, "Christ whole and entire, God and man, becomes present." In the case of sacramentals, however, the manner of Christ's presence, apart from not being of a substantial kind, depends by and large on the *opus operantis Ecclesiae*. That is why our perception of the real presence in sacramentals, especially the minor blessings, is not as vivid as in the sacraments.

The foregoing theological consideration can be summed up thus: Sacramentals are liturgical celebrations whose subject are Christ and the Church. Stated in other words, the sacramentals have three principal dimensions: symbolic, Christological, and ecclesiological. The symbolic dimension refers to the aptitude of the rite, which is normally made up of formularies, gestures, and material elements, to signify the effects of sacramentals. The Christological dimension points to the presence of Christ and his paschal mystery, which is the fount from which the sacramentals draw their power of sanctification. Lastly, the ecclesiological dimension underlines the Church's intercessory role and the communal character of the celebration.

The second point needing closer examination is how sacramentals are related to the sacraments. As *SC* 60 has pointed out, one of the purposes of the sacramentals is to dispose the faithful to receive the chief effect of the sacraments. The relationship does not stop there. Just as the other sacraments do not operate independently of the basic sacraments of baptism and the Eucharist—indeed all the sacraments except penance may be celebrated within the Mass—so no

11. Paul VI, *Mysterium fidei*, no. 39; English text in *Documents on the Liturgy, 1963–1979* (Collegeville, 1982) 385. Henceforth *DOL*.
12. S. Marsili, "La liturgia presenza di Cristo," Anamnesis 1 (Casale Monferrato, 1988) 94. The translations from Italian are mine.

sacramental is celebrated without reference to one or the other sacrament. As we shall have the occasion to point out later in this chapter, religious profession is closely linked to baptism, the rite of funerals alludes to both baptism and Eucharist, and the dedication of a church and an altar consists essentially in the celebration of the Holy Eucharist in the new building. Even sacred objects like holy water remind the faithful of the sacraments. Thus the sacramentals not only prepare the faithful for the celebration of the sacraments, they also engrave in their memory the moments of encounter with Christ through the sacraments.

The third point that needs to be discussed in greater detail is the role sacramentals play in the life of the individual faithful and the community as a whole. According to SC 61, together with the sacraments, sacramentals are able to sanctify "almost every event" in human life. The conciliar commission has interpreted this to include not only the "state of life" such as virginity but also the various events that occur in the lives of people.[13]

Sacramentals relate to the different cycles of human life and activities. Although their importance with respect to the sacraments is secondary, they occupy a fairly large portion of the faithful's normal existence. They allow Christ and his paschal mystery to be really present in the ordinary and daily circumstances of life. The innumerable blessings that accompany people in their personal, family, and social life and in their daily work and struggles are a remarkable proof of the importance people normally attach to sacramentals. The *Book of Blessings*, for instance, contains rites for various blessing such as of families, children, elderly people, new home, library, office and shops, gymnasium, tools, animals, and fields.[14] Its predecessor, the tenth-century *Romano-Germanic Pontifical*, has a much wider range of blessings. It has a blessing for practically anything that people use, including bathing soap and, alas, instruments of ordeal, as well as any place where people gather or work.[15]

SC 61 has made the observation that by means of the sacraments

13. *Schema, modus* 3, no. 24, p. 10.
14. *De benedictionibus* (Vatican City, 1984). Henceforth *DB*.
15. C. Vogel, ed., *Le Pontifical romano-germanique du dixième siècle* (Vatican City, 1963) 2: 320–421. Henceforth *PRG*.

and sacramentals "there is hardly any proper use of material things that cannot be directed toward human sanctification and the praise of God." In a sense, this is more readily achieved through the sacramentals. For while the sacraments use exclusively such elements as water, bread and wine, and oil, the sacramentals cover a wider area consisting of places and objects: homes, shops, farms, tools, food, and objects of devotion. Thus, not only do sacramentals sanctify almost every event in the life of the faithful, they also endow material things with divine meaning and purpose: everything can be directed toward human sanctification and the praise of God.

These, then, are the theological principles that should serve as premises to the inculturation of sacramentals, namely the liturgical nature of sacramentals as actions of Christ and the Church; their purpose in relation to the sacraments; and the place they hold in the various turning points of human life as well as in the events both great and small that happen in the life of individual Christians and their communities.

The Cultural Principles. Inculturation, we pointed out in the first chapter of this work, is like lighting a candle simultaneously at both ends. One end is what the typical editions and the official documents propose. The other end is what culture is able to offer. The Constitution on the Liturgy is keenly aware of and, to a point, wary of the role culture plays in the formation of the rites of the sacraments and sacramentals. *SC* 62 embodies such sentiment: "With the passage of time certain features have crept into the rites of the sacraments and sacramentals that have made their nature and purpose less clear to the people of today; hence some changes have become necessary as adaptations to the needs of our own time."[16]

Although the council focused its discussion on the sacraments, the framers of this article had surely in mind the sacramentals as well. Hence the observation made regarding the undesirable cultural features that had crept into the liturgy of the sacraments has relevance to the liturgy of sacramentals. We need only to remember the medie-

16. The historical background and meaning of *SC* 62 is discussed in A. Chupungco, *Liturgies of the Future: The Process and Methods of Inculturation* (New York, 1989) 104ff.

val blessing of the instruments of ordeal. The people's cultural sensitivity in the tenth century did not disdain the use of the primitive and shocking means of ordeal to determine the guilt or innocence of accused persons by submitting them to painful tests, like walking on blazing gridiron or being thrown into a deep well. The *Romano-Germanic Pontifical* contains formularies to invoke divine approval for the use of such instruments and for the bizarre practice itself.[17]

Other examples where we find cultural interference are the rites of exorcism of some objects and places for the purpose of driving away the evil spirits or demons who were believed to inhabit them. Exorcisms of this type have cast a long shadow upon the chief meaning of blessing as an act of thanking God for his gifts.[18] Popular belief in demonic inhabitations, which was deep-seated in the worldview of medieval society, had a measurable influence on the formularies for the blessing of salt and water.[19] Some sacramentals are at times connected with questionable if not outright superstitious beliefs and practices. In some places holy water is believed to drive the devil away and protect people from lightning; objects of devotion like medals are ascribed with healing and apotropaic power.

The point *SC* 62 wanted to make is that the sacramentals, because of their intimate connection with the people's culture and traditions, have undergone changes in the course of time that did not always prove congenial to their nature and purpose. Since some sacramentals, more than many of the sacraments, are frequently inserted into daily life, they tend to be more vulnerable to the infiltration of culture. We are not implying that culture is directly responsible for every ill in the institution of sacramentals. However, it is not likely to find a sacramental, particularly a blessing, that has no cultural basis or at least some cultural allusion underneath.

The *Apostolic Tradition* of Hippolytus of Rome contains ordinances for the institution of widows, lectors, virgins, subdeacons, and healers and for the celebration of various blessings. The institution of lectors and subdeacons is not necessarily cultural in origin, but the

17. *PRG*, 2: 380–394. The *Pontifical* carries also a blessing of weapons for war on p. 378.
18. A. Triacca, "L'esorcismo," Anamnesis 7, pp. 169–191.
19. *PRG*, 2: 152–154.

institution of widows, virgins, and healers and the rite for the blessing of evening lamps and fruits leave no doubt as to their cultural roots.[20] The *Romano-Germanic Pontifical* carries formularies for the blessing of cheese on Holy Saturday and of lamb, meat of other animals, and milk and honey on Easter Sunday.[21] The pastoral cycle and the season of spring as well doubtless inspired the blessing of these objects at this time of the year. The *Book of Blessings* has retained the rites for the blessing of animals, fields, and flocks and for the offering of the first harvest in obvious consideration of the agricultural and pastoral cycle.[22]

After making the observation that the negative features of culture that were assimilated by sacramentals have made their nature and purpose less clear for the people of today, SC 62 issues the call for an urgent review of the rite of sacramentals, keeping "the needs of our own times" in mind. The call is faithfully echoed by SC 79. When sacramentals are reviewed in the light of the primary criterion of active participation, "the conditions of our own days must also be considered." The Constitution on the Liturgy is not telling us that the liturgy should refrain from further contacts with culture in order to avoid falling into the mistakes of the past. There are enough liturgical principles and norms to safeguard the integrity of Christian worship. What it tells us is that the rites of the sacramentals need to be updated so that the faithful may participate more actively in them.

Far from downplaying the incontestable role of culture, the Constitution on the Liturgy suggests that our success in updating the liturgy of the sacramentals and promoting active participation will depend on how we involve culture in the process. To update means to adapt to the present-day culture, and to promote active participation means, among other things, to foster a keen awareness of the cultural dimensions present in the celebration. In short, the renewal of the liturgy of sacramentals cannot be considered apart from culture, and its adaptation can be understood only within the framework of inculturation.

20. Hippolytus of Rome, *Apostolic Tradition*, ed. B. Botte (Münster, 1963) 30–32, 60–80.
21. *PRG*, 2: 369, 115–116.
22. *DB*, chs. 21, 22, and 23, pp. 279–299.

The Pastoral Principles. The overriding principle of the liturgical reform and hence of inculturation is embodied in the declaration of *SC*
14: "The Church earnestly desires that all the faithful be led to that
full, conscious, and active participation in liturgical celebrations called
for by the very nature of the liturgy." It follows that "in the reform
and promotion of the liturgy, this full and active participation by all
the people is the aim to be considered before all else." *SC* 79 gave
concrete shape to this principle when it decreed that the liturgy of
the sacramentals should be reviewed "in the light of the primary criterion that the faithful participate intelligently, actively, and easily."[23]

Active participation is the pastoral principle pervading the entire
program of conciliar reform. It underlies every conciliar legislation on
the revision of liturgical rites and texts. The liturgy of the Mass, the
other sacraments and sacramentals, the Divine Office, the liturgical
year, as well as music, arts, and furnishings, should be revised or reexamined in view of active participation. *SC* 63's provision for the
use of the vernacular in the celebration of sacramentals is in reality
nothing more than a logical application of the innovative *SC* 36,2:
"The use of the mother tongue in the administration of the sacraments and sacramentals can often be of considerable help for the
people," that is, for active participation.[24] Likewise, the provision of
SC 63b concerning the preparation of particular rituals should be
read in the context of the principle of active participation: "These rituals are to be adapted, even in regard to the language employed, to
the needs of the different regions."

Besides putting emphasis on active participation, *SC* 79 introduced
three new legislations to meet other pastoral needs. These are the introduction of new sacramentals, the reduction in the number of reserved blessings, and the permission for laypersons to administer
some sacramentals. As regards the first, *SC* 79 makes the following
provision: "When rituals are revised, in accord with art. 63, new sacramentals may also be added as the need for them becomes appar-

23. G. Shirilla, *The Principle of Active Participation of the Faithful in*
"Sacrosanctum concilium" (Rome, 1990).
24. For a more extensive discussion of *SC* 36,2 and *SC* 63 see A. Chupungco,
"The Translation, Adaptation, and Creation of Liturgical Texts," *Notitiae* 208
(1983) 695–707.

ent." The question was raised during the conciliar debate whether this text empowered local bishops to introduce new sacramentals for their respective Churches. The proposed text, which had not cited SC 63, seemed to imply that the power was reserved to the Holy See. It will be remembered that canon 1145 of the 1917 Code decreed that the Apostolic See alone could introduce new sacramentals and change or abolish existing ones. In answer to the query the conciliar commission added to the final text the phrase "in accord with art. 63" and clarified the issue with this explanatory note: since SC 63 deals with particular rituals over which the conferences of bishops have responsibility, it would be up to them to institute new sacramentals as occasion might arise.[25]

There is a supporting reason for this change of policy. Sacramentals are by nature and purpose closely linked with the daily life of the faithful. Sometimes they have been occasioned by concrete human situations from which they also derive their relevance. It is, of course, true that some sacramentals, like the dedication of a church and the rite of funerals, have universal or cross-cultural value. However, a great number of sacramentals, especially the blessings, are deeply rooted in the traditions and culture of a particular people. A quick glance at the medieval Franco-Germanic blessings will make us realize that these are a faithful and picturesque description of the cultural life, social habits, worldview, and preoccupations of the Franco-Germanic people. In contrast, the sacraments, except penance and anointing of the sick, produce only a blurred portrait of how these people lived. In short, since the purpose of sacramentals is to accompany the faithful in those areas of daily life with which the sacraments are not directly concerned, it is the duty of the local bishops to identify such areas and to institute the apposite or appropriate sacramentals. It is obvious that here we are dealing more with liturgical creativity than with inculturation.

The second innovation introduced by SC 79 deals with the issue of limiting the number of reserved blessings. The issue is clearly a pastoral concern for some local Churches. The text of SC 79 reads: "Reserved blessings shall be very few; reservations shall be in favor only of bishops and Ordinaries." The conciliar commission made the ob-

25. *Schema, emendationes* 7 (Vatican City, 1963) 17, 24.

servation that the reservation of certain blessings to particular ministers has made it cumbersome for the faithful to obtain them. In large dioceses and in mission territories bishops are often restricted in their movement. For this reason SC 79 has called for a reduction in the number of reserved blessings, and this in favor of local bishops. On its part the conciliar commission expressed the opinion that the blessings to be reserved to the bishops should be those that touch directly the life of the entire diocese.

A related question raised during the council was whether reservations should be in favor of bishops only or whether they should be extended to other Ordinaries like the major religious superiors. As many as 121 council Fathers opted to limit the reservations to the bishops, but the final vote favored the inclusion of other Ordinaries. The conciliar commission interpreted the vote to mean that the "Ordinaries of the religious will continue to keep the faculties they enjoy under the present law for their subjects and in places pertaining to the jurisdiction of their religious order."[26]

The third innovation introduced by SC 79 can be regarded, at least during the council, as one of the more significant changes in the liturgy in favor of lay ministers. At the request of two council Fathers the conciliar commission formulated the following paragraph: "Let provision be made that some sacramentals, at least in special circumstances and at the discretion of the Ordinary, may be administered by qualified laypersons." After this emendation had been favorably voted upon, 153 Fathers submitted a *modus* asking nonetheless for its suppression. Other *modi* wanted the various circumstances to be enumerated and the kind of laypersons, such as religious laybrothers and parents, to be specified. The bill of lay participation in the Church did not sail through the council without resistance.

To all the objections the conciliar commission gave two answers. First, "in the text the principle is admitted that by the nature of sacramentals they are not reserved to clerics, and that the church can depute a layperson to give a blessing in the name of the church." In support of this the commission brought forward the example of allowing lectors, who are in fact laypersons, to bless bread and fruits. "Hence priestly power," according to the conciliar commission, "is not

26. Ibid., *modus* 3, nos. 8–10, p. 7.

required for every blessing." Second, "since the scope of the Constitution on the Liturgy is to enunciate basic principles, specific matters concerning sacramentals and the circumstances and conditions of their administration are to be relegated to the decision of the post-conciliar commission." Regarding the plea for setting down precautions to minimize abuse, the commission noted that practically every word or phrase in this paragraph is in itself a precaution: "some sacramentals," "in special circumstances," "at the discretion of the Ordinary," "may be administered," and "qualified laypersons."[27]

Thus the Constitution not only set forth the right and duty of the faithful to participate actively in liturgical celebrations, it also empowered laypersons to administer some sacramentals. Indeed, it is not stretching the point to say that lay liturgical ministry is already implied in the principle of active participation. Laypersons are enjoined not only to respond to prayers, sing, and interiorize the meaning of the liturgical celebration but also to serve the community as liturgical ministers. At the time of the council this was considered an exceptional concession to laypeople. Today, with the institution of special ministers of Communion and the Sunday celebration in the absence of a priest, the debate regarding the liturgical ministry of the laity, which was quite lively during the council, has let off much steam.

Looking back at the council discussion, we perceive a shift in the pastoral direction of the Church. The council was slowly submitting to the inevitable: the Church had to abandon the tradition of an exclusive clerical liturgy. Beneath the conciliar commission's declaration that "the priestly power is not required for every blessing," we read an urgent message. The worldwide decline in priestly vocations has a detrimental effect on the effectiveness of the Church's spiritual ministry. The council became clearly aware of the need to engage the laity in active liturgical ministry. Surely the administration of at least some of the sacramentals was something the Church could no longer deny qualified layleaders.

From the conciliar document we gather the following pastoral principles to guide the work of revising the liturgy of sacramentals and adapting them to the conditions of our own day: the active participation of the faithful, the institution of new sacramentals as the need

27. Ibid., 19.

for them becomes apparent, less restriction on the authorized minister of sacramentals, and a greater involvement of laypersons in liturgical ministry.

The Constitution on the Liturgy singled out for its consideration three sacramentals: the consecration of virgins, religious profession, and the rite of funerals. As regards the first, which is celebrated nowadays with extreme rarity, all that the council had to say is contained in the standard formula: "The rite for the consecration to a life of virginity as it exists in the Roman Pontifical is to be revised." Religious profession (SC 80) and the funeral rite (SC 81–82), however, received considerable attention from the framers of the Constitution and from the council Fathers themselves.

The Rite of Religious Profession. The preparatory commission in charge of religious profession made some rather poignant remarks on the rites then currently used by religious communities, especially of women. It reported that a variety of particular rituals existed for the vesting and profession of candidates to religious life. It bemoaned the fact that some communities simply adopted the rite for the consecration of virgins, while others, neglecting altogether the liturgical sense of the celebration, used rites based solely on devotional practices. A good number of bishops and prelates thus urged the council "to put some order into these ceremonies and lay down norms to safeguard their dignity and unity." To solve the confusion caused by an unrestrained sense of singularity found among several religious institutes, the commission suggested that a common rite for religious profession be drawn up that would allow each of the religious institutes to adapt it to its particular charism and character.[28] In this way, the essential unity in the rite of religious profession could be achieved without loss to the individual character of each religious family.

To lay stress on the nature of religious profession as an act of consecration to God, the preparatory commission also suggested that it be celebrated within the Mass, "like the consecration of virgins and

28. Ibid., *emendationes 7*, Appendix: *declarationes*, p. 29.

practically all the other rites for the consecration of persons."[29] The Constitution on the Liturgy actually contains similar provision for the rite of confirmation (*SC* 71) and the rite of marriage (*SC* 78). The reason for integrating these rites with the Mass varies from rite to rite. Confirmation, which includes the renewal of baptismal vows, is conferred within the Mass to evoke the traditional plan of Christian initiation. Marriage is normally celebrated within the Mass to show the relation of the covenant between wife and husband to the sacrificial offering of Christ on the cross.[30] In the case of religious profession, the reason for integrating it with the Mass seems to be in order to highlight its consecratory character.

The final text of *SC* 80 incorporates the suggestions of the preparatory commission. It reads: "A rite of religious profession and renewal of vows shall be drawn up with a view to achieving greater unity, simplicity, and dignity. Apart from exceptions in particular law, this rite should be adopted by those who make their profession or renewal of vows within Mass. Religious profession should preferably be made within Mass."

In passing, it may be pointed out that the phrase "apart from exceptions in particular law" is not clear. When some council Fathers, presumably belonging to religious orders, requested that it be interpreted officially to mean "without injury to particular rites," the commission answered that it was a matter for the postconciliar commission to decide. What appears to be underneath this *modus* was the anxiety over the possible fate of the particular rites of profession once the typical edition had been published. The same sentiment is present in another *modus*, which asks that "the plan of the rite should be drawn up in order to preserve unity, but there should be freedom in individual applications."[31] These details bear a special message. They tell us that while unity in essentials is the ultimate goal we should diligently pursue, a measure of diversity in the way the local communities live out the essentials is in itself an essential trait of unity.

29. Ibid., 25.
30. The background of *intra missam* in *SC* 71 and 78 is discussed in Chupungco, *Liturgies of the Future*, 112–113, 121.
31. *Schema, modus* 3, p. 20.

In the light of the conciliar discussion we get a clearer insight on the meaning attached by *SC* 80 to the revision of the rite of religious profession. Its insistence that there should be greater unity in the rite was a timely response to a preconciliar situation of disorder and lack of liturgical orientation among several rites of profession. However, several council Fathers felt that unity should not become detrimental to long-standing and praiseworthy traditions proper to each religious order and congregation. Even in the rite of religious profession there should be enough room for diversity and adaptations. This becomes increasingly relevant today, because religious institutes are returning to the original charisms of their founders and hence to their particular traditions. Furthermore, the phenomenal expansion of religious institutes outside their place of origin, particularly in countries outside the Western Hemisphere, has made their members sensitive and alert to each other's cultural differences.

The Rite of Funerals. The preparatory commission devoted considerable attention to the revision of the funeral rites. Before presenting its recommendations it made a judicious evaluation of the rite being used before the conciliar reform. Among other things it underlined the following points. First, "the concept of death that emerges from the formularies does not bring out the doctrine of hope held by the church on Christian death." Second, "some elements, particularly the responses and readings, are too frightful and distressing." And third, "the faithful present during the rite are not mentioned in the prayer of the church."[32] We need only to recall the solemn and dramatic sequence *Dies irae* or the anguished cry *Libera me, Domine*, both of them fiercely intent on sowing terror and desperation in the heart of every faithful, to understand the criticism of the preparatory commission. Likewise the exclusive attention bestowed by the *Tridentine Missal's* formularies to the soul of the dead made the Church forget to pray for the bereaved. In fairness to this *Missal*, however, we should admit that it includes some magnificent and spiritually uplifting antiphons, such as *In paradisum* and *Ego sum resurrectio*. It also includes the sense of filial piety in the formularies for the deceased

32. Ibid., *emendationes* 7, Appendix: *declarationes*, p. 29.

parents of the priest, who prays that he may be reunited with them in heaven.[33]

To correct the defects of the current rite of funerals the preparatory commission proposed the following points. First, "the funeral rites should have more texts that speak of the paschal meaning of Christian death." Second, there should be "greater variety of Mass formularies, especially the readings, for the increment of faith." Third, "the active participation of the faithful should be fostered through suitable means." And fourth, "the funeral customs among various peoples, especially in the missions, should be respected and introduced into the Christian rite, as long as they are not superstitious."[34]

SC 81 incorporates all these recommendations. The text reads: "The rite of funerals should express more clearly the paschal character of Christian death and should correspond more closely to the circumstances and traditions of various regions. This applies also to the liturgical color to be used." The provision on color was belatedly added at the request of some council Fathers. Although the original text sufficiently implied this, they considered it opportune to mention explicitly the possibility of adopting the funeral colors of the place. The question of which color to use may appear today as a matter of secondary importance, but at the time of the council the departure from the traditional liturgical color scheme was regarded as a progressive move. Color scheme is an important ingredient of culture, but the council did not wish to focus all its attention on it. We should not forget that native funeral rites have other, more significant elements, like the plan of the celebration and the various ritual gestures and symbols that accompany the rite.

The provision of the Constitution on the Liturgy for the revision of the rite of funerals applies to the preparation of particular rituals based on the typical edition. The provision is formulated in two articles. First, the funeral rite should express the paschal character of Christian death, and second, it should be adapted to the funeral traditions of various regions. We may say that the two are inseparable; they check and balance each other. With these articles the Constitution sets down in effect the principle that the assimilation of local fu-

33. *Missale Romanum* (Tournai, 1961) 116–140.
34. *Schema, emendationes 7,* Appendix: *declarationes,* p. 29.

neral customs must not override the paschal dimension of the Christian rite, its sense of hope in the resurrection, and trust in the love and mercy of the Creator. It is possible that in a number of today's secularized societies death has lost its religious meaning and the rites for the dead do not even allude to the other dimensions of human life. But the Constitution makes it likewise clear that the paschal dimension of death must not cancel out the local expressions of grief and mourning. The liturgy must not be allowed to become insensitive to the manifestations of human emotions.

INCULTURATION ACCORDING TO THE TYPICAL EDITIONS

It will be recalled that in the first chapter of this work we referred to the typical editions as one of the points of departure in the process of inculturation. The other is the people's set of cultural patterns. The process of inculturation means that these two points meet in order to produce an inculturated liturgical rite. In this section of our study we focus our attention on a number of the typical editions of sacramentals with a view to formulating some basic liturgical principles of inculturation. Apropos, A. Bugnini's posthumous book, *The Reform of the Liturgy, 1948–1975*, offers excellent background reading on the work of the Consilium in charge of the revision of the sacramentals. His report covers the areas of the ministries, religious profession, the rite of funerals, consecration of virgins, dedication of a church and an altar, and the blessing of oils.[35]

The introduction to the typical edition of each of the sacramentals, especially when it carries a section on adaptation, deserves particular consideration. Sacramentals differ by and large from each other in nature, purpose, and liturgical structure. There is, for example, hardly any notable similarity between the dedication of a church and the rite of funerals. And though the various rites of blessings follow the same pattern, they are often unrelated in scope and purpose. But it is not impossible to draw from the different rites some general principles of inculturation that are applicable to every sacramental. Apart from this, each typical edition contains the particular norms and suggestions on how the rite can be adapted or inculturated. It is beyond

---

35. A. Bugnini, *The Reform of the Liturgy, 1948–1975* (Collegeville, 1990) 727–802.

the scope of this chapter to discuss in detail how each and every sacramental, especially the blessings, can be inculturated. It would be too taxing and not kindly to do so. However, in the course of the discussion we shall refer frequently to some typical examples of sacramentals for concrete presentation and application.

From among the general principles enunciated in the typical editions the following stand out for their scope and application: the essential elements constituting the rite, the importance of the word of God, active participation, and the influence of culture.

The Constitutive Elements of the Rite. Inculturation, which is not the same as creativity in the strict sense of the word, is a sure way of conserving and perpetuating liturgical tradition. It will be recalled that inculturation is a type of dynamic translation that allows the original message to be conveyed according to the people's cultural pattern. Inculturation means retaining the sound tradition of the liturgy and keeping the way open to legitimate progress. To this effect SC 23 cautions: "A careful investigation is always to be made into each part of the liturgy to be revised." Careful investigation involves the tedious work of identifying the essential elements of a liturgical rite.

No one will claim that it is absolutely necessary to preserve every sacramental instituted by the Church. In fact, some sacramentals come and go, depending on their usefulness to the local Church and on the culture of the people onto which they are grafted. Apotropaic exorcism, for example, was a familiar sacramental in the life of the medieval Church because of the prevailing worldview it had. Today it is celebrated with extreme rarity and restraint. We are, however, dealing with the work of inculturation, which requires that the essential elements of sacramentals be preserved; otherwise, their original meaning would be changed or simply lost. Change or loss of the meaning and purpose of sacramentals does not exactly fit in the concept of inculturation; it would be more appropriate in this case to speak of creativity.

An example that can illustrate the point regarding the need to identify the essential components of a rite is the dedication of a church. Its celebration is lavish in ceremonies that are rich in symbolic evocation. The following ritual elements give to the celebration a sense of grandeur, solemnity, and drama: the ceremony of handing over the church to the bishop by those who have been involved in its building; the sprinkling of the people, the walls of the church, and the altar; the deposition of the relics of the saints; and the traditional rites of anointing the altar and the walls of the church, burning the incense on the altar, incensing the nave, and covering and lighting the altar.[36]

The foregoing rites, whose symbolism the typical edition scrupulously explains, do not constitute the essence of the rite of dedication. Even the rites of anointing, incensing, and covering and lighting the altar are not constitutive elements, even if liturgical tradition has attached special meaning and force to them. That is why if weighty reasons stand in the way these traditional rites may be omitted. But the thing to remember about inculturation is not the possibility of omitting but of translating tradition into the living culture of the people. Since the elements of the rite of dedication have cultural underpinnings, they can be translated through the method of dynamic equivalence into other cultural patterns. What the typical edition suggests concerning the matter is noteworthy: "The conferences of bishops may adapt this rite, as required, to the character of each region, but in such a way that nothing of its dignity and solemnity is lost."[37]

What is the essential element of the dedication of a church? The typical edition answers this with absolute conviction. Although the tradition of the Church in both East and West assigns a special prayer of dedication, "the celebration of the Eucharist is the most important and the one necessary rite for the dedication of a church."[38] There is no other sacramental that claims the Eucharist as its constitutive element. The typical edition explains this rather unusual feature, saying that "the celebration of the eucharistic sacrifice achieves the end for which the church was built and the altar erected." Furthermore, "the Eucharist, which sanctifies the hearts of those who receive it, in a sense consecrates the altar and the place of

---

36. *Ordo dedicationis ecclesiae et altaris* (Vatican City, 1977). Henceforth *ODEA*. English text of the introduction in *DOL*, 1369–1387. See L. Chengalikavil, *The Mystery of Christ and the Church in the Dedication of a Church* (Rome, 1984).

37. *ODEA*, no. 18; *DOL*, 1374.

38. *ODEA*, no. 15; *DOL*, 1373.

celebration."³⁹ For this reason, "the celebration of the Mass with the proper preface and prayer for a dedication must never be omitted."⁴⁰

The typical edition thus vindicates the original concept of the church as a building designed primarily for the Eucharistic celebration, no matter whether it is also used for other purposes or how culture has influenced its architectural form in the course of time. The celebration of the Mass is the chief element of the rite, which declares that the church and its sacred furnishings are effectively dedicated, that is, set apart for the end for which the building has been erected, namely the celebration of the Eucharist. Thus, any proposal to inculturate the rite of dedication must always include the celebration of the Mass. What inculturation means in effect is that the rites and texts of the Mass as well as the explanatory rites are made to speak to the people in language and symbols that signify their way of consecrating, setting apart, and dedicating something of value to God.⁴¹

Another example is the rite of religious profession.⁴² The result of the study made by M. Augé on the typical edition shows that "while the new rite for religious profession intentionally took inspiration from the ancient monastic rituals in order to 'codify,' so to speak, in the new rituals of religious families the authentic tradition regarding content and structure, it nonetheless presents itself as a ritual model." Augé considers the following elements to be part of liturgical tradition and hence should not be easily disregarded in the process of inculturation: the celebration of profession before the offertory of the Mass, the deposition of the formula of profession on the altar, and the wording of the suggested formula of profession.⁴³

The typical edition encourages religious families to "adapt the rite so that it more clearly reflects and manifests the character and spirit

---

39. *ODEA*, no. 17; *DOL*, 1374.

40. *ODEA*, no. 18; *DOL*, 1374.

41. For background reading on the process and method of inculturating the liturgy of the Mass see Chupungco, *Liturgies of the Future*, 56–101.

42. *Ordo professionis religiosae* (Vatican City, 1975). Henceforth *OPR*. English text of the introduction in *DOL*, 1019–1023. See A. Nocent, "Monastic Rites and Religious Profession," *The Church at Prayer* (Collegeville, 1988) 3: 285–309; M. Augé, "La professione monastica e religiosa," Anamnesis 7, pp. 47–63.

43. Augé, "La professione monastica e religiosa," Anamnesis 7, p. 63.

of each institute."[44] The text does not explicitly address the question of inculturation. But it would not be overly stretching one's imagination to include the word "culture" in the phrase "character and spirit of each institute." We know for a fact that cultural factors have deeply affected the history of religious institutes. Today they continue to influence their character and spirit because of the cultural diversity among their members. Thus, the work of adapting the rite of profession so that it may clearly manifest the "character and spirit" of a particular institute is inconceivable without inculturation.

An inculturated rite of religious profession not only in different institutes but also in the different houses of the same institute in various parts of the world will be marked by the traditional symbols used in the locality to express consecration to God. It is no longer feasible or suitable to produce a uniform rite of profession for international use. The history of the rite informs us that a number of cultural elements entered into the shaping of the rite of religious profession in consideration of the different cultural backgrounds of the persons who joined religious life. Augé mentions among these the *stipulatio* of the Roman law and the *immixtio manuum* of the feudal system.[45] The bottom line is that the rite of religious profession, like all the other liturgical rites, is always inured to the "incursions" of culture, because the character and spirit of a religious institute are in fact influenced by cultural realities.

Apart from the foregoing cultural considerations, there are norms pertaining to the nature of the rite to which the typical edition directs our attention. The first of these is the clear distinction between the three chief stages of religious life, namely the novitiate, first profession, and final profession. The typical edition explains that "since all these rites have their own special character, each demands a celebration of its own. The celebration of several rites within the same liturgical service is to be absolutely excluded."[46] The second norm speaks of the need to keep the character of the entrance to the novitiate restrained and simple to forestall any moral pressure on the novice. This should take place outside the Mass. The third norm wishes

44. *OPR*, no. 14; *DOL*, 1022.
45. Augé, "La professione monastica e religiosa," 51–52.
46. *OPR*, no. 8; *DOL*, 1022.

to safeguard the liturgical distinction between perpetual and temporary profession or renewal of vows: "What is proper to one rite may not be inserted into another."[47]

Underlying the requirement to distinguish liturgically the three different rites is an important theological consideration. Religious life is a gradual process by which men and women dedicate themselves to God and to the Church according to the spirit of the evangelical counsels. It is a process that in some way imitates the steps of Christian initiation from the time of the catechumenate up to the celebration of the initiatory sacraments. There is, at any rate, a close relation of religious profession and the sacrament of baptism. In the words of LG 44: "As baptized Christians the religious are already dead to sin and dedicated to God; but they desire to derive still more abundant fruit from the grace of their baptism. For this purpose they make profession of the evangelical counsels in the church."

Seen in this light, religious profession manifests the nature of sacramentals in bearing a kind of resemblance to baptism and disposing men and women to receive its chief effect. We should not wonder why religious profession has been called a "second baptism." Some monastic rituals in circulation before the conciliar reform dramatize this concept of a second death and resurrection. They direct the newly professed to lie prostrate covered with black cloth and surrounded by four candles, while the church bells toll. Before Communion the deacon intones the verse from Ephesians 5:14, which says, "Awake, O sleeper, and arise from the dead, and Christ shall give you light." For eight days thereafter the newly professed wore the monastic cowl in obvious imitation of the neophytes, who in patristic times wore the baptismal robe for eight days until the *Dominica in albis* (*deponendis*).

The third example to illustrate the need for determining what is essential for each sacramental can be drawn from the rites of blessings. The *Book of Blessings* is remarkably clear on this point: "In the adaptation of celebrations a careful distinction should be made between matters of less importance and those principal elements of the celebrations that are here provided, namely, the proclamation of the

47. OPR, no. 4; DOL, 1019–1020; OPR, no. 14; DOL, 1022.

word of God and the church's prayer of blessing. These may never be omitted even when the shorter form of a rite is used."[48]

The proclamation of God's word and the prayer of the Church constitute the essence of a blessing. Many people consider persons, places, and things duly blessed if the minister makes the sign of the cross over them, even without uttering a word, and sprinkles them with holy water. The typical edition tells us that these outward signs are not essential to the rite of blessing. Nevertheless, they bring to mind the saving acts of God, express the relationship of sacramentals to the sacraments, and dispose the faithful to participate actively in the celebration of the rite. The typical edition enumerates the traditional outward signs to accompany the rite of blessing: stretching out the hands or raising or joining them, laying on of hands, making the sign of the cross, sprinkling with holy water, and incensing.[49] There is hardly any need to stress the fact that these signs are cultural symbols that can be dynamically translated into corresponding local symbols in order to enhance the significance of the various rites of blessings and foster lively participation.

In this connection it would be useful to remember that certain societies ban certain symbols on grounds of morality and the observance of good manners. Typical is the laying on of hands on the head of a person. In places where it is considered a social taboo, an appropriate dynamic equivalent will have to take its place. Conversely, in some places where there is a strong Catholic tradition it would take an enormous effort to convince people that the use of holy water, candles, and incense is not necessary. Some are distressed and others feel they are cheated when the priest does not sprinkle with holy water the people, places, and objects he blesses. Ministers should be warned that certain gestures, like the sign of the cross and the laying on of hands, and objects, like holy water and candles, have been appropriated by some Catholics for superstitious ceremonies. These outward signs of blessing, especially the sign of the cross, can be re-

48. *DB*, no. 23, p. 16. For background reading on the rites of blessing see P. Jounel, "Blessings," *The Church at Prayer*, 3: 263–284; A. Triacca, "Le benedizioni 'invocative' in genere e su 'persone,' Anamnesis 7, pp. 113–152; Idem, "Le benedizioni 'invocative' su 'realtà cosmiche,'" ibid., 153–166.

49. *DB*, nos. 25–26, p. 16.

garded in themselves as forms of preaching the gospel and of expressing the faith. But since they are so easily prone to be employed for superstitious purposes, the typical edition ordains that "to guard against any danger of superstition, it is not ordinarily allowed to impart the blessing on objects and places merely through an outward sign and without the word of God or a prayer."[50]

The typical edition underlines the importance of the two constitutive parts of the rites of blessings, namely the word of God and the prayer of praise and petition. These, according to the typical edition, determine the nature and purpose of the blessing itself. It declares that the celebration of the word of God "ensures that the blessing is a truly sacred sign, drawing its meaning and efficacy from the word of God itself." After the council the proclamation of the word of God finally became an integral part of the liturgy of sacraments and sacramentals. But in the case of blessings, it is also a constitutive element that transforms them into liturgical actions.

The other constitutive element, namely the prayer of blessing, consists in divine praise and petition for help through Christ in the Spirit. The typical edition explains that the central point here "is the formulary for blessing, or the prayer of the church which is accompanied by special outward signs." The prayer of blessing expresses the role of the Church in the celebration of sacramentals. When the typical edition defines the prayer of blessing as the prayer of the Church, it invokes the doctrine of *ex opere operantis Ecclesiae*.[51]

In conclusion, we may sum up the discussion by stressing the need to determine, before we embark on the work of inculturation, which elements are constitutive of the nature and purpose of sacramentals and which elements are merely accessory to the rite. The essential elements themselves vary from one sacramental to the other, but it is not a formidable task to identify them, because of what the typical edition has to say or what information we can gather about their origin and nature. In saying that certain elements of sacramentals are nonessential, we do not mean to express disinterest for them. Often they play truly key roles in the inculturation of the liturgy, because

50. Ibid., no. 27, p. 17.
51. Ibid., nos. 20–22, p. 15.

they have close affinity to culture and can be replaced more easily by equivalent cultural elements.

The Place of the Word of God. The introduction to the second edition of the *Order of Readings for Mass* opens with a theological discourse on the place of the word of God in liturgical celebrations. It highlights *SC* 7's declaration that in the liturgy Christ "is present in his word, since it is he himself who speaks when the holy Scriptures are read in the Church." In the liturgy the word of God acquires life and efficacy by the power of the Holy Spirit. At the same time it serves as a foundation of the liturgical action. The introduction quotes the following passage from article 4 of the Decree on the Ministry and Life of Priests: "The proclamation of the word is required for the sacramental ministry itself, since the sacraments are sacraments of faith, which draw their origin and nourishment from the word." The word of God and the sacraments are inseparable, especially in the celebration of the Eucharist.[52] One of the conclusions of the Strasbourg Congress in 1958 heralds this conciliar doctrine: "It is not enough to say that the Bible occupies a privileged place in the liturgical celebration. It plays such a fundamental role that without the Bible there would be no liturgy."[53]

The liturgy rightly reserves a privileged place for the word of God in the celebration of the Eucharist and the other sacraments. But we should not forget that God speaks to his people and Christ still proclaims his gospel also in the celebration of sacramentals. In fact, since sacramentals lack the *ex opere operato* efficacy of the sacraments, which, strictly speaking, can be administered without the Liturgy of the Word, and, alas, this happens regularly in the rite for reconciliation of individual penitents, they derive their meaning and efficacy from God's word alone through the intercession of the Church. That is why the celebration of the sacramentals, if done outside Mass, normally includes the proclamation of God's word. In the case of blessings, the word of God, as we have seen early on, is a constitutive element of the liturgical celebration itself.

The place of God's word in the liturgy of sacramentals receives

---

52. *Ordo lectionum Missae* (Vatican City, 1981) nos. 1–10.
53. *The Liturgy and the Word of God* (Collegeville, 1959) v.

particular attention from the introduction to the *Rite of Funerals:* "In any celebration for the deceased, whether a funeral or not, the rite attaches great importance to the readings from the word of God. These proclaim the paschal mystery, they convey the hope of being gathered together again in God's kingdom, they teach remembrance of the dead, and throughout they encourage the witness of a Christian life."[54] Short of defining the word of God as the constitutive element of Christian funerals, the text sums up the effects that flow from the proclamation of God's word. The word of God injects into the celebration for the dead a profound Christian meaning. Through the word of God the rite of funerals expresses the Church's faith in the power of Christ's death and resurrection, hope of eternal life, devotion toward the dead, and the obligation to live genuine Christian lives.

Thus the word of God becomes, so to speak, a proclamation of the Church's doctrine on Christian death. But in the rite of funerals the Scripture is not only proclaimed, its Book of Psalms is also prayed. With regard to this the typical edition explains that in its offices on behalf of the dead "the Church turns again and again especially to the prayer of the psalms as an expression of grief and a sure source of trust." In clear distinction from the prayer formularies, which are basically a profession of faith and a prayer of intercession for the deceased and the bereaved, the psalms allow the faithful to experience in the liturgy those human emotions often denied them by the euchological formularies. Although the other sacramentals also use the psalms, the rite of funerals assigns to them a special role in the celebration because of the sentiments of loss and hope they are able to convey.

We meet a similar emphasis on the word of God in the rite of religious profession. The introduction to the typical edition has a timely reminder about the function of the word of God: "The liturgy of the word for the rite of profession can be an important aid to bringing

---

54. *Ordo exsequiarum* (Vatican City, 1969) no. 11, *DOL*, 1070. Henceforth *OE.* See R. Rutherford, *The Death of a Christian* (New York, 1980) 111–146; D. Sicard, "Christian Death," *The Church at Prayer*, 3: 221–240; and P. Rouillard, "I riti dei funerali," Anamnesis 7, pp. 195–227.

out the meaning of religious life and its responsibilities."[55] There is no doubt as to the exceptionally rich content of the prayer formularies used in the rite of profession. They articulate and communicate a theology and spirituality that give value to the consecrated life. The solemn blessing at the rite of perpetual profession, which ably joins catechesis to prayer and religious life to salvation history, is a magnificent example of this. Yet these formularies do not exhaust the theology of religious life. The typical edition reminds us that also the biblical readings can be an important aid to understanding the nature and purpose of religious life. The formularies, however sublime and rich in content, do not say everything. The word of God has always something more to say.

Obviously much work was put into the choice of biblical passages that the typical edition proposes for the celebration of religious profession. For this reason, the typical edition makes an exception to the rule by allowing one reading from the special list of readings for the rite of profession when the ritual Mass for the day of religious profession may not be used, though the exception does not apply on great solemnities. The proposed readings from the Old and New Testaments have been carefully chosen to address the topics of religious vocation, service, community life, and Christian discipleship.[56] Though the formularies, including the proper prefaces, also deal with these topics, the word of God has a particular way of articulating them and imparting the message: it is a sacrament that gives meaning and efficacy to sacramentals.

We discussed at some length the place of the word of God in the liturgy of blessings. We saw that the proclamation of God's word is an integral part of the rites of blessings and hence should not be omitted. It is God's word that transforms the blessings into sacramentals, into genuine liturgies where God speaks to the people. That is why the models offered by the *Book of Blessings* always propose biblical readings to suit the nature of the blessing. These are meant to shed light on the meaning of each blessing and to connect it with an aspect of salvation history. Choosing at random any verse from

55. *OPR*, no. 10; *DOL*, 1022.
56. *DOL*, 83–87.

85

the Bible does not do justice to the particular role the word of God plays in the celebration of blessings.

To sum up the discussion we may say that in the liturgy of sacramentals the word of God sheds light on the doctrine proposed by the Church; in some way the word of God becomes also a proclamation of what the Church believes, whereas in the Book of Psalms, the word of God offers to the Church inspired prayers for various occasions; the word of God becomes an expression of what the Church and its members experience at particular moments in life.

How does this affect the inculturation of sacramentals? The postconciliar typical edition of various sacramentals has seriously considered which biblical readings and psalms to propose for each celebration in an effort to convey through them both doctrine and human sentiments. Thus, in the process of inculturating the sacramentals, not only the prayer texts but also the proposed biblical readings and psalms should be examined in order to determine which doctrine and human sentiments emerge from the liturgical rite. After all, the prayer formularies do not say it all, and inculturation should not even be started if there is only limited information regarding the nature and purpose of each sacramental. But apart from this consideration, the work of inculturation should give an effectively prominent place to the word of God in the liturgy of sacramentals. For in the final analysis it is the word of God that confers a Christian dimension on the elements assimilated by the liturgy from culture and traditions. Where, for example, should the proclamation of the word be inserted in the plan of the celebration? What reading and listening techniques and what symbols and ritual gestures are available to enhance the unique role of the word of God in the celebration of sacramentals?

Active Participation. The third principle governing inculturation is active participation. *SC* 79 instructs that "the sacramentals are to be reviewed in the light of the primary criterion that the faithful participate intelligently, actively, and easily." The postconciliar books for the celebration of sacramentals observe this conciliar norm rather strictly. The *Book of Blessings* explicitly calls attention to the principle of active participation as one of the foremost considerations for the planning of a blessing.[57]

Active participation, however, requires the presence of an assembly. The typical edition of the *Book of Blessings* returns again and again to this requirement as it stresses the importance of communal celebration. The following are some of the points raised by the typical edition. First, communal celebration is in some cases obligatory, but in every case it is more in accord with the character of liturgical actions to hold communal celebrations. Second, the diocesan or parish community should assemble, with the bishop or pastor presiding, for the more important blessings that concern the diocese or the parish. Third, the blessing of things or places should not take place without the participation of at least some of the faithful. For the *Book of Blessings*, active participation means the presence of an assembled community, however small in number. The insistence on presence and communal celebration seems to be based on the representational character of the liturgy. Even when there is no assembly of the faithful, the person for whom the blessing is celebrated and the minister should keep in mind that "they represent the church in the celebration."[58]

The principle of active participation can be more easily realized in the celebration of sacramentals because their liturgy allows more room for variations in regard to the ritual plan and the role of the minister and the assembly. This last point needs elaboration. The hierarchical nature of the liturgy—and this includes the sacramentals— requires a clear distinction of roles in the celebration. The presidential or other ministerial functions, even if these are exercised by laypersons, always have reference to the hierarchical order of the liturgy. "Hierarchical" in this context does not mean the actual presidency of an ordained minister but the distinction between the one who presides and the assembly over whom the minister presides.

In effect, what this means is that the liturgical assembly is distinguished from the ministers, even if these are laypersons, who hold the function of proclaiming the word of God and invoking divine blessing in the name of the Church. The *Book of Blessings* gives the

57. *DB*, no. 24, p. 16.
58. Ibid., nos. 16–17, pp. 13–14.

theological foundation for this hierarchical distinction: "The ministry of blessing is joined to a particular exercise of Christ's priesthood and is performed according to the state and office proper to each one," namely the bishop, presbyters, deacons, and instituted acolytes and lectors, and, in virtue of the common priesthood, also other laymen and laywomen.[59] To drive the point, the same book suggests that the solemn celebration of blessings should be planned in such a way that a deacon, reader, cantor, and choir will be able to fulfill their respective functions.[60]

Active participation is stressed in varying degrees by the other typical editions for the sacramentals. The *Rite of Funerals,* for instance, envisages for the significant times between death and burial "the gathering of family and friends and, if possible, of the whole community to receive in the liturgy of the word the consolation of hope, to offer together the eucharistic sacrifice, and to pay last respects to the deceased by a final farewell."[61] The typical edition likewise encourages laypersons to lead the usual psalms and prayers at the stations at home and at the cemetery when there is no deacon or priest present.[62] As regards the hierarchical character of the celebration, the typical edition reminds all members of the community "that to each one a role and an office is entrusted: to relatives and friends, funeral directors, the Christian community as such, finally, the priest, who as the teacher of faith and the minister of comfort presides at the liturgical rites and celebrates the Eucharist."[63]

To conclude, active participation, which is presented by *SC* 79 as the primary criterion for the revision of the rite of sacramentals, should be regarded also as the primary criterion for the work of inculturation. It is not enough for the liturgy of sacramentals to don the vesture of culture and traditions, it should be planned in such a way that the faithful can participate intelligently, actively, and easily in the celebration. We should add that active participation is not con-

59. Ibid., no. 17, p. 13.
60. Ibid., no. 24, p. 16. For background reading on the role of laypersons see Bugnini, "The Laity and the Liturgy," *The Reform of the Liturgy,* 752–762; P.-M. Gy, "La fonction des laïcs dans la liturgie," *La Maison-Dieu* 162 (1985) 43–54.
61. *OE,* no. 3; *DOL,* 1069.
62. *OE,* no. 5; *DOL,* 1069; see also nos. 19 and 22,4 on deputing laypersons.
63. *OE,* no. 16; *DOL,* 1071.

fined to verbal responses or to the singing of psalms and hymns. Ritual actions as well as other symbolic expressions connected with sacramentals are also effective means to bring about active participation. Lastly, it should be remembered that active participation, as envisaged by SC 79, cannot be dissociated from the culture and traditions of the people. Active participation has a dimension which is pronouncedly cultural.

The Influence of Culture. SC 39 names the sacramentals among the liturgical rites wherein the conferences of bishops are free to make adaptations. *SC* 79 prescribes that when the sacramentals are revised, "the conditions of our days must also be considered." Since sacramentals are on the whole closely linked with human life and activities, culture has an important contribution to make in the shaping of their liturgical rite. For sacramentals belong basically to the category of signs, and hence to the realm of culture, even though they are in reality sacred signs that signify effects, particularly of a spiritual kind, and sanctify various occasions in human life.

In view of this cultural consideration, a good number of the typical editions for the sacramentals carry norms on how the culture and traditions of each region can suitably be admitted into the celebration. Given its prevalently cultural dimensions, the *Rite of Funerals* is evidently a fine example of how sacramentals relate to culture. The introduction to the typical edition offers the following advice: "In such matters as family traditions, local customs, burial societies, Christians should willingly acknowledge whatever they perceive to be good and try to transform whatever seems alien to the Gospel."[64] The study made by D. Sicard on the funeral liturgy of Latin Christians before the Carolingian reform throws light on the role of culture in the formation of the rite.[65] C. Vogel also offers enlightening information on how the ancient Church adopted Roman funeral cus-

64. *OE*, no. 2; *DOL*, 1068. See the case study on the relationship between cultural practices and Christian tradition by T. Pereira, *Towards an Indian Christian Funeral Rite* (Bangalore, 1980).

65. D. Sicard, *La liturgie de la mort dans l'Église latine des origines à la réforme carolingienne* (Münster, 1978); idem, "The Funeral Mass," *Reforming the Rites of Death*, Concilium 32 (New York, 1968) 45–52; ibid., "Christian Death," 236–240; see also P. Rouillard, "I riti dei funerali," Anamnesis 7, pp. 203–209.

toms. Some of these, according to Vogel, are the white tunic for the dead, the use of the *feretrum*, the funeral cortege or *exsequiae*, the manner of burial or *depositio*, the eulogy or *laudatio funebris*, and the celebration of the funeral banquet called *refrigerium*.[66]

The typical edition of the *Rite of Funerals* recognizes that different conditions and funeral traditions do exist in local Churches. For this reason it presents three models for a funeral, leaving it to the conferences of bishops to prepare particular rituals that will suit the needs of local Churches. To assist them the typical edition lays down particular norms for the adaptation of the rite. These norms appear also in the typical editions of the other liturgical books like marriage and Christian initiation.

Three of these norms are particularly relevant to our subject. First, it is up to the conferences of bishops "to weigh carefully and prudently which elements from the traditions and culture of individual peoples may be appropriately admitted and accordingly to propose to the Apostolic See further adaptations considered to be useful or necessary that will be introduced into the liturgy with its consent." Second, the conferences of bishops may "retain elements of particular rituals that may now exist, provided they are compatible with the Constitution on the Liturgy and contemporary needs, or to adapt such elements." And third, the said conferences are enjoined "to prepare translations of the texts that are truly suited to the genius of the different languages and cultures and, whenever appropriate, to add suitable melodies for singing."[67]

In addition to these general norms of adaptation, the typical edition calls attention to certain Christian funeral practices that may need to be reexamined in the light of local cultural traditions. It passes to the conferences of bishops the responsibility "to decree, whenever pastoral consideration dictates, omission of the sprinkling with holy water and the incensation or to substitute another rite for them." Though sprinkling and incensation are eloquent symbols of what the Church professes when it celebrates the funerals, they do

---

66. C. Vogel, "L'environnement cultuel du défunt durant la période paléo-chrétienne," *La maladie et la mort du chrétien dans la liturgie* (Rome, 1975) 381–413.

67. *OE*, no. 21; *DOL*, 1072. For a discussion of these modes of adaptation see Chupungco, *Liturgies of the Future*, 125–154.

not possess cross-cultural values. Hence they can become pastorally irrelevant in places where they have no roots in native funeral tradition. The typical edition likewise leaves to the conferences of bishops the decision "to decree for funerals the liturgical color that fits in with the culture of the peoples, that is not offensive to human grief, and that is an expression of Christian hope in the light of the paschal mystery." In the West black is traditionally associated with mourning, but in other parts of the world, like China, white is the color of grief. The provision of the typical edition answers the question raised during the council regarding the appropriate color for funeral liturgy, considering the differences in the color scheme of various regions.[68]

The question, what is in a color? betrays an attitude of indifference to an aspect of culture that means so much to mourners. In situations when sensitivities run high it is best to abide by what is regarded as standard. To express the Pentecostal aspect of death, red was once used for the funeral Mass for a priest, and the church was decorated with red flowers and banners. The reaction of the assembly was one of cultural shock and offense, although the intention of the liturgy planners had been theologically sound. Color scheme is such a sensitive element of culture that the liturgy cannot disregard it without the risk of cultural alienation.

A contemporary model for adapting the typical edition is the *Order of Christian Funerals*, prepared for its member conferences of bishops by the International Commission on English in the Liturgy.[69] Its translation of several Latin formularies can, without hesitation, be classified under the category of dynamic equivalence. The opening line of formulary 125B, which translates *Inclina, Domine, aurem tuam ad preces nostras*, is an excellent example of what dynamic equivalence can achieve: "Lord, in our grief we turn to you. Are you not the God of love who open your ears to all?" Aside from translated texts, the *Order of Christian Funerals* includes several original formularies that express the theology of death and capture the human feelings caused by death. Some of the formularies are sublime in their articulation of faith and emotion: "Grant that we may hold his/her mem-

68. *OE*, no. 22, 5–6; *DOL*, 1073.
69. ICEL, *Order of Christian Funerals* (Washington, 1985).

ory dear, never bitter for what we have lost nor in regret for the past, but always in hope of the eternal kingdom where you will bring us together again." The formulary for a young person unravels our unspoken, at times resentful, bewilderment: "We grieve over the loss of one so young and struggle to understand your purpose."[70]

In consideration of local customs prevailing around the different parts of the English-speaking world, the *Order of Christian Funerals* provides useful alternatives and suggestions for the ritual plan of the celebration. It carefully explains the meaning of such traditional symbols as the Easter candle, holy water, and incense and suggests the use of other, additional symbols like the pall, the Book of Gospels, the cross, and fresh flowers.[71] The commendable effort of ICEL to inculturate the language and, to some extent, the symbols of the rite of funerals shows that inculturation is not the exclusive domain of local Churches outside the Western Hemisphere. Obviously, in places where funerals are held with strikingly elaborate, ornate, and colorful ritual, the product of inculturation will likewise be characterized by drama and exuberance. But inculturation should not be equated with such qualities. It is, as we have noted early on in this work, rather a matter of how successfully the liturgy assimilates a people's cultural pattern of thought, language, rites, and artistic forms.

As regards the cultural aspect of blessings, P. Jounel makes this observation: "More than any other liturgical book, the Book of Blessing must take local traditions into account. Many of the rites of blessing proposed in the typical edition will be useless for most countries; on the other hand, some countries will look in vain for formularies that they would find very useful. The needs of a primarily agrarian civilization are not those of an industrialized region."[72] Progress in technology, like rainmaking, has made some of the agricultural blessings appear anachronistic, even to farmers themselves. Jounel notes poignantly that the traditional blessings adapted to modern situations seem artificial to many. He asks with amusement, "The blessing of horses gave rise to picturesque processions, but how can the same happen

70. Ibid., 67, 342.
71. Ibid., nos. 35–38, pp. 10–11.
72. Jounel, "Blessings," *The Church at Prayer*, 3:278.

with tractors?"[73] Inculturation, however, does not require the rites of blessings to be dramatic and colorful in order to be meaningful and relevant. As Jounel himself points out, "It is still more important to recognize before we use things to our advantage, that all of them, even after they have been transformed by human genius, come ultimately from God and derive an unfailing goodness from him."[74]

Inculturation deals directly with cultural patterns rather than with rites and other forms of cultural manifestation. Hence the inculturation of the rites of blessing would mean that the Christian spirit of thanking God for the gifts, "which earth has given and human hands have made," is given a new cultural expression following the people's pattern of thinking and speaking about divine gifts rather than their traditional and at times already obsolete rites and symbols. In themselves blessings are not anachronistic, though some of their forms are no longer meaningful. Blessings, which acknowledge God as the ultimate giver of everything that is good, are relevant even in today's technological world. The question is how the cultural pattern of a local Church captures and expresses the genuine spirit of blessing.

CONCLUSION

The area of interest covered by this chapter is what the Constitution on the Liturgy and the various typical editions for sacramentals present as the theological, pastoral, and cultural principles of inculturation. Our study led us to examine also the possibilities of inculturation offered by the typical editions, especially of the rites of blessing, religious profession, the dedication of a church, and funerals. So much can be done to make these sacramentals more relevant to the life of local communities and the individual believer.

But it would not be in keeping with the spirit of the council and the liturgical books to think that all we need to do is inculturate existing sacramentals. A good number of these were instituted as a response to the needs of local Churches at some particular moment. Their relevance to the life of a Christian community or an individual is on the whole contingent on changing circumstances. Sacramentals

73. Ibid., 284.
74. Ibid.

are so deeply rooted in the concrete reality of life that the long and short of it is that they come and go. That is why their inculturation should not be regarded as the final goal of liturgical renewal. There will be occasions when a local Church will experience the need for new sacramentals, for new forms of God's continuing presence in the rhythm of daily life outside the sphere of the sacraments. The council anticipated this when, with characteristic spirit of pastoral discernment, it decreed that new sacramentals may be introduced by conferences of bishops as the need for them may arise.

Whether we deal with the inculturation of existing sacramentals or with the creation of new ones, the declaration of SC 60 serves as our basic guide: "The church has instituted sacramentals. These are sacred signs bearing a kind of resemblance to the sacraments: they signify effects, particularly of a spiritual kind, which are obtained through the church's intercession. They dispose people to receive the chief effect of the sacraments and they make holy various occasions in human life."

Chapter Three

Popular Religiosity and Liturgical Inculturation

LITURGY AND POPULAR RELIGIOSITY

A decade after the council, liturgists began to focus their attention, as an afterthought, on popular religiosity. In the seventies several Churches in Latin America and Europe, particularly in Italy, France, and Spain, witnessed the blossoming of literature on this subject. In 1979 F. Trolese compiled in a bibliography on popular religiosity, as many as 528 titles written mostly during the decade.[1]

The Effect of Liturgical Renewal on Popular Religiosity. It would seem that the interest of liturgists up till the seventies had been confined to the task of implementing the postconciliar liturgical reform. In the late sixties and early seventies the typical editions of liturgical books were revised and published with great regularity. In 1968 the rite for the ordination of deacons, presbyters, and bishops was published. This was followed in 1969 by the rites of infant baptism, marriage, and funerals; in 1970 by the *Roman Missal* and Lectionary and the rites of religious profession and consecration of virgins; in 1971 by the books of the Liturgy of the Hours and the rites of abbatial blessing and the blessing of oils; in 1972 by the rites of adult initiation, confirmation, and anointing of the sick; in 1973 by the rite for instituting lectors and acolytes; in 1974 by the rite of penance; and in 1978 by the rite of dedication of a church and altar.

During those years local Churches all over the world received the

---

1. F. Trolese, "Contributo per una bibliografia sulla religiosità popolare," *Ricerche sulla religiosità popolare* (Bologna, 1979) 273–325. Trolese's bibliography covers for the most part the Italian, French, and Spanish. In the German-speaking world the following liturgists are to be mentioned: B. Fischer, "Liturgie und Volksfrömmigkeit," *Liturgisches Jarhbuch* 17 (1967) 129–143; W. Heim, "Volksfrömmigkeit und Liturgie," *Heiliger Dienst* 21 (1967) 17–29; J. Baumgartner, ed., *Wiederentdeckung der Volksreligiosität* (Regensburg, 1979).

new typical editions with such frequency that there was no moment of respite from the work of translating and adapting them. Pastors needed material for catechesis and for planning the celebration of the liturgy according to the newly revised rites. Liturgists had their hands full. In an effort, which was truly praiseworthy, to direct the attention of the faithful to the liturgy as the summit and fount of Christian life, liturgists and pastors zealously banned popular devotions during liturgical celebrations. The time allotted for the holy hour, novena to the patron saint, and the common recitation of the rosary in church was turned over to Bible services or the Liturgy of the Word. In places where the faithful clung tenaciously to popular devotions, like the novena to Our Lady of Perpetual Help, some pastors improvised a practical solution: they readily integrated the novena with the Mass. On the whole these concerted efforts allowed the liturgy to regain the place of importance it rightly holds, but the healthy balance between liturgy and popular religiosity suffered in the process.

The Constitution on the Liturgy itself gave little attention to the question of popular religiosity. *SC* 13 limited itself to that one aspect on which the liturgy has a direct bearing, namely the *pia exercitia*, or popular devotions. And it dealt with the question as an appendage to the conciliar theology of the liturgy, which assigns the liturgy as the summit and fount of the entire activity of the Church. Indeed, as *SC* 7 solemnly declares, the liturgy is considered as an exercise of Christ's priestly office. Hence, no other activity of the Church can compare with it in dignity and efficacy. *SC* 13 rightly concludes that by its very nature as the priestly act of Christ to which he associates the Church, the liturgy far surpasses any of the popular devotions. As P. Visentin regretfully acknowledges, "it may appear strange, but we have to admit clearly and honestly that the question regarding popular religiosity, which is very alive today, was more or less inexistent during Vatican II and even in the course of the preparatory work of the liturgical reform."[2]

This appendant treatment of popular religiosity on the part of the council should not come as a surprise. The classical liturgical movement that shaped the conciliar document was concerned primarily

2. P. Visentin, "Liturgia e religiosità popolare: due mondi ancora lontani?" *Liturgia e religiosità popolare* (Bologna, 1979) 219. Translations from Italian are mine.

with the promotion of the liturgy and liturgical life. The rediscovery of the place the liturgy holds in the mission and spiritual life of the Church led to the radical restructuring of prayer life. Against all odds and violent criticisms, the liturgical movement sharply distinguished between what is liturgical and hence essential to the life of the Church and what is not. That is why the Constitution on the Liturgy is entirely devoted to the liturgy and to things liturgical. Except for a passing mention of popular devotions, the Constitution has nothing to say about popular religiosity as an expression of Christian worship. Such dichotomy was the unfortunate effect of a full-swing reaction to a then prevailing situation in which the value of the liturgy was often eclipsed by popular religiosity. Thus, the liturgical movement and the council cut down to size the importance enjoyed by popular religiosity among the faithful.

The Reappraisal of Popular Religiosity. The afterthought appraisal of popular religiosity seems to have been brought about by two factors. The first was the rediscovery of the value popular religiosity had, not only for the promotion of the Latin American liberation theology but also for the integrity of Christian worship. It began to dawn upon liturgists that the integral worship of the Church consists of both the official and the popular forms of prayer. In fact, *SC* 12 itself teaches that "spiritual life is not limited solely to participation in the liturgy." There are, besides the liturgy, other forms of worship. Apropos, E. Cattaneo remarks that "liturgical piety as well as popular devotions have existed without interruption from the beginning of Christianity until now, and both of these will always continue to exist."[3]

Commenting on *SC* 12, S. Marsili observes: "In the church there are two forms of worship enjoying the same right, at least on the practical level: one is organized and commanded by the authority of the church to be observed by all, the other which is varied, undefined, and changeable arises from the people."[4] Although Marsili makes a neat distinction between the liturgy as the worship *by* the Church and popular devotions as worship *in* the Church, he suggests

3. E. Cattaneo, "Proposta di uno schema sui rapporti fra la liturgia e pietà popolare nella Chiesa occidentale," *Liturgia e religiosità popolare*, 79.
4. S. Marsili, "Liturgia e non-liturgia," Anamnesis 1 (Turin, 1974) 151.

that "every form of prayer which the Christian community performs as church, that is, as body and head or 'a people united with their shepherd,' with the intention of celebrating the mystery of Christ, has the fundamentals of 'liturgy' and can be declared as such."[5]

To this enlightening reflection of Marsili we may add that the prayer life of both the Church and the individual faithful would surely suffer an imbalance should divine worship be confined to the official form. Sacramentals and blessings surely fill those areas of human existence left vacant by the Mass, the other sacraments, and the Divine Office, but they do not fill the need for a more personal and unstructured prayer, which is made available to the faithful by popular religiosity, especially the devotions. In addition, if popular devotions also function as a personal preparation for and an overflow of the experience of God during official worship, they will enhance active participation in the liturgy itself. In other words, the doctrine of *ex opere operato* and *ex opere operantis Ecclesiae* needs the support of personal prayer, which, for some of the faithful, is what the exercise of popular devotions is all about. The fact that the liturgy is the source and summit of the life of the Church only shows that apart from the liturgy there are other activities that make up the total reality of the Church.

The second factor that led to the reappraisal of popular religiosity was the unsettling feeling that the reformed liturgy, even in the vernacular, remained removed from a good number of people who have hitherto worshiped according to one or other form of popular religiosity. For many the official form of worship, especially when no attempt has been made to inculturate it, is helplessly cold and distant. Its classical features, which must have immensely pleased the *homo classicus* of sixth-century Rome, seem to alienate it from the religious experience of assemblies with another worship pattern, particularly of a popular orientation or type. D. Sartore, whose article "Le manifestazioni della religiosità popolare" makes a solid contribution to the topic, writes: "Today we have become clearly aware that this popular phenomenon has values which need to be restudied and that it should become a protagonist in the renewal of the church, which by

5. Ibid., 156.

98

virtue of its mission cannot be reduced to a 'church of the elites.'"[6] For a good number of the faithful, today's revised liturgy with its solemn and exalted language is still very much an exclusive activity of the elite group in the Church. If it is not injected with the qualities of popular religiosity, it can in time become an endangered species in the life of the ordinary Christian worshiper.

How is popular religiosity to play a leading part in the renewal of a liturgical life that is not reserved to the elite? We receive a partial answer to this question from *SC* 13, which urges that popular devotions should relate to the liturgy, harmonize with the liturgical seasons, and lead the people to the liturgy. *SC* 13 tells us that the liturgy, with its sublime doctrinal content and exquisite form, has enough resources to share with popular devotions. However, it does not tell us how popular devotions can influence the liturgy. It is from the *Document of Puebla* that we receive a complete and satisfactory answer: There should be "a mutual and enriching exchange between the liturgy and popular devotion."[7] Liturgists who write on popular religiosity are unanimous in affirming the need for what *Puebla* describes as a reciprocal relationship between liturgy and popular religiosity.[8]

Although neither *Puebla* nor the liturgists, with the exception of C. Valenziano, use the term inculturation, it is what they advocate in effect. Through the process of inculturation, liturgy and popular religiosity should enter into the dynamic of interaction and mutual assimilation in order to be enriched with each other's pertinent qualities. For local Churches with long-standing popular religious practices

6. D. Sartore, "Le manifestazioni della religiosità popolare," Anamnesis 7 (Genoa, 1989) 234.

7. *Documento de Puebla*, "La evangelización en el presente y en el futuro de América Latina," no. 465 (Buenos Aires, 1979) 167. Translation is mine.

8. For the relationship between liturgy and popular religiosity see D. Borobio, "Religiosidad popular en la renovación litúrgica: Criterios para una renovación," *Phase* 15 (1975) 345–364; H. Denis, "Les stratégies possibles pour la gestion de la religion populaire," *La Maison-Dieu* 122 (1975) 163–193; Visentin, "Liturgia e religiosità popolare: due mondi ancora lontani?" *Liturgia e religiosità popolare*, 239–246; C. Valenziano, "La religiosità popolare in prospettiva antropologica," ibid., 83–110; J. Castellano, "Religiosidad popular y liturgia," *Nuevo diccionario de liturgia* (Madrid, 1987) 1730–1743; and Sartore: "Le manifestazioni della religiosità popolare," 245–246.

it would seem that inculturation is the only available solution to the problem of liturgical alienation and also the best method to transform popular religiosity into an authentic vehicle of the gospel.

There can be no doubt as to what the contact between the official form of worship and popular religiosity can bring about. It will give a more human countenance to the liturgy and a more solid theological and ecclesial foundation to popular religiosity. In the words of the *Document of Puebla:* "We should encourage a mutual and enriching exchange between the liturgy and popular devotion, so that the yearning expressed in prayer and charisms, which is present in our countries today, may be channeled with clarity and prudence. On the other hand, popular religiosity, with its wealth of symbols and expressions, can share its creative dynamism with the liturgy. With due discernment such a dynamism can help to incarnate better in our culture the universal prayer of the church."[9]

INCULTURATION AND THE FORMS OF POPULAR RELIGIOSITY

The process of inculturation requires a close examination not only of the parts of the liturgy to be modified or changed but also of the elements of popular religiosity to be admitted into the liturgy. Since inculturation means reciprocity, the liturgy should remain open to the influence of popular religiosity. Obviously the question we have to address is whether popular religiosity has the linguistic and ritual resources that can be availed of by the liturgy, and how these can enrich the shape of the liturgy, so that the faithful who are at home only with popular religiosity can begin to feel at home also with the Church's official form of worship.

A Definition of Popular Religiosity. Sartore defines popular religiosity as "a set of spiritual attitudes and cultic expressions which are variedly connected with the liturgy."[10] His definition concurs with J. Evenou's concept of popular religiosity as "a collection of behaviors and ritual practices that are more or less in harmony with the pre-

9. *Documento de Puebla,* no. 465, 167–168.
10. Sartore, "Le manifestazioni della religiosità popolare," 232; see A. Terrin, "Religiosidad popular y liturgia," *Nuevo diccionario de liturgia,* 1722–1730.

scriptions of the hierarchic authorities."[11] Sartore makes an important clarification on the term "religiosity." Today, he writes, the word "religiosity" should not be taken as the equivalent of subjective religion nor of a degenerate form of it. Religiosity is rather a concrete form of genuine religion, even if its expressions are at times found lacking in sound doctrine and ecclesiastical discipline.[12] The word "popular," however, is an appellation whereby religiosity is distinguished from the liturgy or official form of worship. We should note that the word "popular" is not an evaluation of the popularity a celebration is able to command from the people. Depending on the region, certain liturgical celebrations, especially those that include rites rooted in popular tradition like the Palm Sunday procession and the veneration of the cross on Good Friday, do have a strong popular appeal, whereas some forms of popular religiosity, again depending on the region, may receive little or no interest from the people.

The nature and forms of popular religiosity are such that the ecclesiastical authority does not and can not always exercise direct supervision over its manifold expression. This situation does sometimes create among Church officials an attitude of ambivalence toward popular religiosity, an ambivalence whose spectrum ranges from acceptance to outright rejection. We must admit though that some forms of popular religiosity connected with baptism, marriage, and funerals are of ambiguous character. In them the borderline between the genuinely religious and the purely social, between orthopraxis and superstition, is not always clearly delineated. A good number of popular devotions, however, carry the seal of ecclesiastical approval. Evenou concisely sums up the long history of the Church's reaction to popular religiosity in these words: "The attitude of the Church to popular religion has varied, in different periods and countries, from a tolerance meant to show receptivity to a weakness that lets itself be overrun as, at the other extreme, a severity that condemns and seeks to purge."[13]

The *Directory on the Pastoral Ministry of Bishops* issued in 1973 by

11. J. Evenou, "Processions, Pilgrimages, Popular Religion," *The Church at Prayer* (Collegeville, 1988) 3:256.

12. Sartore, "Le manifestazioni della religiosità popolare," 232.

13. Evenou, "Processions, Pilgrimages, Popular Religion," 256.

the Congregation of Bishops gives balanced and prudent advice on how bishops are to deal with popular religiosity. They should "not forbid any of the good and useful things belonging to the popular celebrations and amusements occurring in the course of the year on feasts proper to a place or of the universal calendar (e.g., those of a patron saint or the Blessed Virgin Mary, Christmas, Easter, etc.)." The *Directory* calls on bishops to perfect these practices and properly orient their religious aspects, imbuing them with sound faith, supernatural devotion, and Christian doctrine. Accordingly, the bishops must guard against expressions of popular religiosity that conflict with Christian doctrine or the mind of the Church. They must eliminate such expressions, but at the same time they should "prudently open the way to new forms of devotion."[14]

Forms of Popular Religiosity. Authors have different ways of classifying the forms of popular religiosity. The groupings made by Sartore can be considered standard. He classifies them under four categories: first, devotions to Christ, the Blessed Virgin, and the saints in the form of pilgrimages, patronal feasts, processions, popular devotions, and novenas; second, the rites related to the liturgical year; third, traditional practices in conjunction with the celebration of the sacraments and other Christian rites like funerals; and fourth, institutions and religious objects connected with various forms of popular religiosity.[15]

"Popular devotion" is the English translation of the Latin *pia exercitia.* Among the forms of popular religiosity, it carries the distinction of being encouraged by the Church. Current ecclesiastical legislation identifies the following forms of popular devotion among those that should "be reverently preserved and spread among Christian families and communities," namely the rosary, stations of the cross, and certain novenas that precede liturgical solemnities like Pentecost and Christmas.[16]

Although several countries in Europe and Latin America can claim

14. No. 90c. English text in *Documents on the Liturgy, 1963–1979* (Collegeville, 1982) 837. Henceforth *DOL.*
15. Sartore, "Le manifestazioni della religiosità popolare," 232–233; see Valenziano, "La religiosità popolare in prospettiva antropologica," 94–95.
16. *Directory on the Pastoral Ministry of Bishops,* no. 91; *DOL,* 838.

to be the centers of popular religiosity,[17] the Philippines as a former colony of Spain shares and preserves faithfully, in modified form, much of its colonizers' religious traditions. As the foremost Filipino historian, H. de la Costa affirms that the Filipino religious culture as we know it today began with the coming of the first Spanish missionaries.[18]

In order to give additional information on those forms of popular religiosity that could eventually enter into the dynamic of interaction with the liturgy, it would be useful to describe here briefly some of the Filipino forms of popular religiosity.[19] Since a good number of these forms were actually brought along by the Spanish missionaries, most of the examples given below are not original to the Philippines, though they have put on local color and character. The *cenaculo*, or passion play during Holy Week, originated in medieval Europe, while the *encuentro* at dawn of Easter Sunday is still kept in southern Italy and in some countries of Latin America. Practically all the popular devotions in the Philippines come from Europe.

The forms of popular religiosity in the Philippines may be grouped, somewhat differently from the classification made by Sartore, under the following categories: popular devotions, processions, altars or shrines, and religious drama and dance. In practice these forms overlap or are intertwined. Popular devotions are often performed during processions and in front of altars; religious dance sometimes accompanies street processions; religious drama may be an expression of personal and community devotion. In several instances these activities are undertaken by individual persons, a group, or even an entire community as a votive offering in fulfillment of a religious vow or as an act of thanksgiving for divine blessings.

Most of the popular devotions in the Philippines, as in the other parts of the Christian world, bear the seal of the Church's approval. The more common of these are visits to the Blessed Sacrament, holy

17. A. Nesti, "La religiosità popolare in America Latina: Problemi di ricerca," *Rassegna di teologia* 3 (1990) 247–268.

18. H. de la Costa, "Religious Renewal: An Asian View," *Philippine Studies* 20 (1972) 93–94.

19. See A. Chupungco, *Towards a Filipino Liturgy* (Manila, 1976) 78–93; idem, "Folklore and Christian Worship," *Boletin eclesiastico de Filipinas* 47 (March–April 1973) 166–171.

hour devotions, novenas, the Angelus, and the recitation of the rosary. There are also seasonal devotions, such as the stations of the cross in Lent, pilgrimages to Marian shrines, especially in the month of May, and *visita de iglesias*, or prayer before the Blessed Sacrament on the night of Holy Thursday and the greater part of Good Friday. *Visita de iglesias* is generally a family or group affair. In large cities like Manila, it is customary to visit—most people do it on foot—a minimum of seven churches and spend moments of prayer before the altar of reposition. This religious ritual, which always draws a throng of people, is probably the Philippines' most moving and edifying expression of Eucharistic devotion.

Indigenous to the Philippines is the chanting before home altars during Lent or, less frequently, at funeral wakes, of the verses of the *Pasyon*. The *Pasyon* is a book written in seven major Filipino languages consisting of 3,150 rhymed stanzas of five lines each. Though it narrates the history of salvation from the moment of creation to the second coming of Christ, including apocryphal stories, much of it is a detailed account of and a prayerful meditation on the passion of Christ. Friends and neighbors drop in to sing a portion of the *Pasyon* and sit afterward for a meal, which still vaguely retains a sacral undertone.[20]

Processions are a year-round phenomenon. They are held in connection with the feasts and seasons of the liturgical year, during town *fiestas* in honor of patron saints, and in times of calamity and distress, whether natural or man made. Processions, unless they are strictly liturgical, are organized by confraternities and come in various forms. There are street and fluvial processions with sacred images, though a few are without, like the *flores de Mayo*, or the daily offering of flowers, originally by children, to the Blessed Virgin during the month of May. Some processions involve role-playing by persons representing biblical personages, as in *santakrusan*, also in the

20. *Kasaysayan ng Pasiong Mahal* (Manila, 1964). See Maryhill School of Theology, "*Ang Pabasa* and the Liturgy," *The Liturgical Information Bulletin of the Philippines* 9 (March–April 1974) 48–53; R. Ileto, *Pasyon and Revolution* (Manila, 1981); R. Javellana, "*Pasyon* Genealogy and Annotated Bibliography," *Philippine Studies* 31 (1983) 451–467; idem, "Sources of Gaspar Aquino de Belen's *Pasyon*," ibid. 32 (1984) 305–321; idem, *Casaysayan nang Pasiong Mahal* (Quezon City, 1988) 3–42.

month of May, which commemorates the finding of the holy cross. Though *flores de Mayo* and *santakrusan* have degenerated into a beauty pageant and a tourist attraction, they still retain a semblance of religious activity. The procession with the image of the Black Nazarene, or Christ carrying the cross, is held in the district of Quiapo in Manila every January 9 and on Good Friday. It is probably the country's most impressive, but also appalling, procession because of the physical prowess it demands from its jostling all-male participants.[21] The Holy Week processions in the town of Baliuag, north of Manila, with close to a hundred adorned carriages with life-size images, all richly appareled—the carriage for the Last Supper alone has thirteen images—is unbeatably the most exuberant.[22]

Altars, which are an ubiquitous Filipino religious phenomenon, are found in homes, shops, grottoes, vehicles, and at street corners. Altars are places reserved for the veneration of the image of the cross, Christ, and the saints. Most of the public vehicles, called jeepneys, carry altars in honor of Christ and the Blessed Virgin amidst humorous or provocative stickers: a curious amalgam of religiosity, popular wisdom, and playfulness. By far the most popular images are those of the *Santo Niño*, or the Child Jesus, clad in every imaginable outfit; the suffering Christ, or the Black Nazarene; and the Blessed Virgin under every available Marian title. In an attempt to claim the Child as part of human activities and a sharer in the fate of people, the *Santo Niño*, is variously depicted as fisherman, farmer, police officer, or carefree youth. Unlike the sober Roman liturgy, popular religiosity finds no problem about several representations of the same person in one place. Hundreds of the images of the Child Jesus are carried in procession, while home altars are never the monopoly of a single image of the Blessed Virgin.[23]

The *National Catechetical Directory for the Philippines* admits that the Christ of Filipino folk Catholicism is predominantly the *Santo*

21. See B. Beltran, *The Christology of the Inarticulate* (Manila, 1987) 116–124.
22. See G. Casal and R. Jose, "Colonial Artistic Expressions in the Philippines," *The People and Art of the Philippines* (Los Angeles, 1981) 108–111.
23. For background reading on religious images in the Philippines see ibid., 117–121; see also Beltran, *The Christology of the Inarticulate*, 126–135.

Niño, and the suffering Christ.[24] The risen Christ does not occupy as significant a place in the devotional life of ordinary Catholics. In so many words the *Directory* justifies this peculiarity when it points out that "the 'scandal' of both the Infant and the Crucified Christ is grounded in the Good News itself." It observes that a great number of Filipinos see in the Child Jesus the God who made himself accessible, and in the crucified, more than in the risen Christ, a clearer and more powerful sign of God's love. As regards the Filipinos' extraordinary manifestation of devotion to the Blessed Virgin, the *Directory* notes that it is based on the Hispanic roots of Filipino Catholicism as well as on the Filipino society's esteem and respect for women, especially mothers: "a cultural trait fostered and deepened by Christian faith."[25]

Filipino religious culture displays baroque traits in its religious drama and dance. These are held in connection with the liturgical season and town *fiestas.* The following are some of the thriving forms of religious drama in the Philippines. On Christmas Eve the *panuluyan,* or the search for an inn, is held in front of homes. The statues of the Blessed Virgin and Saint Joseph are carried in procession, while a chorus narrates how homeowners sent the holy couple away. The procession enters the church on time for the midnight Mass. In Holy Week the *cenaculo* presents nightly on stage the history of salvation. On Good Friday the *penitensya,* which is a street drama by costumed performers, reenacts the carrying of the cross.[26] At dawn of Easter Sunday several towns hold the *encuentro.* Two separate processions, one with the statue of the risen Christ and the other with a veiled statue of the Blessed Virgin, assemble at the town square to dramatize the meeting of Christ and his mother at dawn of Easter. A young girl dressed as an angel is suspended in midair and lifts the mourning veil of the Blessed Virgin as she sings the anti-

24. *Maturing in Christian Faith* (Pasay City, 1985) no. 41, 34.
25. Ibid., nos. 42–43, p. 35.
26. Ibid., 113–117; see Maryhill School of Theology, "The Christmas Liturgy and *Panuluyan,*" *The Liturgical Information Bulletin of the Philippines* 9 (March–April 1974) 41–47; M. Andrade, "*Encuentro* during Easter Sunday Celebration," ibid., 11 (March–April 1976) 50–52.

phon *Regina coeli.* Then by some mechanism the two statues are made to bow to each other as a sign of Easter greeting.

There are theologians and pastors who object to the practice of the *encuentro,* calling it a distortion of biblical account. R. Brown informs us, however, that from the time of Tatian's *Diatessaron* in the second century there have been elements of a tradition among the Church Fathers, especially those writing in Syriac, like Ephraem, that it was Mary the mother of Jesus, not Mary Magdalene, who came to the tomb early in the morning of Easter Sunday. He cites Loisy, who thinks that this may be the original account, which may have been conformed to the Magdalene tradition of the Synoptics.[27] There is no way we can find out with certainty whether the *encuentro* was inspired by this alternative tradition. But an important consideration to keep in mind is that biblical accuracy is not one of the outstanding traits of popular devotion. And when this is directed to the Mother of God, as in the *encuentro,* devotees require no biblical proof or basis. What the Gospels fail to say, filial piety affirms. Popular devotion simply refuses to believe that Jesus did not appear first to his mother after the resurrection.

Among the traditional religious dances, the more popular are those performed during processions with the image of the patron saint. "Religious" is often a misnomer, since the type of dance merely adopts the traditional folk dance and the music played by the band is not necessarily of a religious kind. There are also a number of dances for a good number of reasons, including the petition of married women for the blessing of fertility. These are performed privately inside the church in front of the images of patron saints. In the month of January the *ati-atihan,* or costume festival of street dancing and merrymaking, is held. Historians trace the practice to the yearly descent of the native Ati to the plains of the island of Panay to receive food in exchange for a dance demonstration. Today it is celebrated in honor of the Child Jesus, who, according to legend, saved the inhabitants from Muslim plunderers. The festival of *ati-atihan* has understandably won the hearts of the devotees of the *Santo Niño* throughout the country. Hundreds of images of the Child

27. R. Brown, *The Gospel According to John, XIII–XXI* (New York, 1970) 981.

Jesus are carried in procession, while dancers, clad like the native Ati, wiggle to the furious beating of drums.

From the foregoing description of the different forms of popular religiosity, we are able to identify the points of encounter and interaction between liturgy and popular religiosity. The more important of these forms are popular devotions, processions, altars, drama, and dance. They vary in their expression, but they possess common traits, which we now examine in view of inculturation.

INCULTURATION AND THE TRAITS OF POPULAR RELIGIOSITY

Inculturation is a process of interaction and mutual assimilation affecting both the liturgy and the different forms of popular religiosity. Here we focus our attention particularly on how popular religiosity can influence the shape of the liturgy. The reverse, which is addressed in part by SC 13 and Pope Paul VI's *Marialis cultus,* nos. 40–55, is fully treated by J. Castellano in an article on the subject.[28]

A "Liturgical" Novena? To illustrate how the liturgy can influence popular devotion it would be useful to cite concrete examples. In conformity with the wishes of SC 13, the Benedictine monks in Manila had the three novenas proper to their Church revised. These novenas are in honor of the *Santo Niño,* Our Lady of Montserrat, and Saint Benedict. The revised version follows a liturgical format: an introductory verse taken from the Divine Office: "O God come to my aid," opening hymn, opening prayer lifted from the Roman Sacramentary, a scriptural reading followed by silence and a short responsory in the style of the Divine Office, proper litany, the prayer of petition, the Lord's Prayer, concluding prayer from the Roman Sacramentary, and a concluding song.[29] The result of the revision is a form of novenas that is as "liturgical" as SC 13 probably envisions them to be. But it is precisely this "liturgical" form that raises a strong feeling of misgiving about the future of such novenas. The florid, discursive, and picturesque quality that is characteristic of popular

28. Castellano, "Religiosidad popular y liturgia," 1739–1741.
29. Abbey of Our Lady of Montserrat, *Devotion in Honor of Sto. Niño* (Manila, 1986); *Devotion in Honor of Our Lady of Montserrat* (Manila, 1985); *Devotion in Honor of Saint Benedict* (Manila, 1979).

devotions is conspicuously absent from them. To what extent can novenas put on the liturgical form without abandoning the features that classify them as popular devotions?

Another example, which at first glance may appear curious, is the novena prayer for Christmas included in L. Lovasik's *Treasury of Novenas*.[30] The formulary is a blend of popular devotion and liturgical texts adapted from the collects and prefaces of Christmas. The following portion of the formulary clearly shows the attempt made by the composer to produce a "liturgical" novena prayer: "Heavenly Father, You made Christmas night radiant with the splendor of Jesus Christ our light. I welcome Him as Lord, the true light of the world. Bring me to the joy of His heavenly kingdom." Another portion reads: "Lord God, I praise You for creating man, and still more for restoring him in Christ. Your Son shares our weakness: may I share his glory." The remaining portions of the novena prayer are lifted from the two prefaces of Christmas: "Father, in the wonder of the Incarnation Your eternal Word has brought to the eyes of faith a new and radiant vision of Your glory" and "No eye can see His glory as our God, yet now He is seen as one like us."

Whatever reservations one might have about the merit of such an approach, it should be weighed together with another consideration. If the liturgy is the summit and fount of popular devotions, should we not expect private prayer to be imbued with the thoughts and words of liturgical texts?

The General Traits of Popular Religiosity. Popular religiosity, according to Sartore, has the following features: "It is bound up with basic human problems and sentiments; it possesses a spontaneous and creative quality, which sometimes puts it at a distance from the doctrine and discipline of the church; it is traditional in orientation; it is often associated with particular places, cultural expressions, social conditions, and the natural disposition of a particular group; it is suited generally for modest and simple people, though it is not necessarily the correlative of social and cultural privation."[31] C. Valenziano describes in synthesis form the qualities that characterize popular religi-

---

30. L. Lovasik, *Treasury of Novenas* (New York, 1986) 31–32.
31. Sartore, "Le manifestazioni della religiosità popolare," 232.

osity: "It is festive, felt, spontaneous; it is expressive, immediate, human; it is communitarian, collective, joyful, symbolic, traditional, alive."[32]

Sartore's characterization of popular religiosity is very useful to our topic. There is, however, one point that as a whole does not apply to every existing form of popular religiosity or to the people concerned. Though he takes issue with A. Gramsci's Marxist view of popular religiosity, he nonetheless regards it as something generally suited for modest and simple people. In the Philippines, at least, a number of popular religious practices belong traditionally to the elite class of society. Examples of these are the processions with privately owned images and richly adorned carriages, the chanting of the *Pasyon*, which always involves the continual serving of food for an entire day, pilgrimages to Marian sanctuaries, and the religious dramas connected with Christmas and Holy Week. The expenses one incurs for these activities are simply beyond the reach of the ordinary townspeople. Thus, Gramsci's interpretation of popular religiosity as a phenomenon of evasion and compensation among the poorer strata of society is called to task by this Filipino phenomenon, where rich and poor alike are involved in the activities of popular religiosity.[33] In reality the rich alone can initiate activities of this proportion.

The foregoing observation is meant to point out that the inculturation of the liturgy with the intention of infusing it with the lively qualities of popular religiosity need not have the unfavorable effect of alienating the elites from the liturgy. The popular form of worship, including such devotions as novenas and the rosary, cannot be regarded quite exclusively as the simple and modest people's domain. In places where the practice of popular religiosity is vibrant, the educated and professional sector of society is not unfamiliar with its phenomena and expressions. That is why the assimilation of the traits of popular religiosity by the liturgy will not necessarily lead to alienation on account of the social standing and educational attainment of people. Rather, the issue will center on one's liturgical up-

32. Valenziano, "La religiosità popolare in prospettiva antropologica," 95.
33. Sartore, "Le manifestazioni della religiosità popolare," n. 4, p. 232. For over a decade A. Gramsci's article "Osservazioni sul folclore," published in 1954, exercised considerable influence on Italian thinking on the subject of popular religiosity.

bringing and preferences. It will probably affect the liturgists more than the elites of the local Church.

Sartore and C. Valenziano mention certain qualities inherent in popular religiosity that should enter the process of liturgical inculturation. These are spontaneity, festivity, joyfulness, and community endeavor. When one considers the forms of popular religiosity that run the gamut from the simplest family rituals to the most elaborate town processions and theatrical presentations, one begins to understand why the liturgy must assimilate the qualities of popular religiosity. Filipinos—and existing documentation on the subject names also the Latin Americans and the people in the south of Spain and Italy—perform certain acts of religiosity with a characteristic flair for drama and with an abandon that verges on recklessness. Here they let loose their pent-up zest for external religious celebration, which the somberness of the official liturgy is quite unable to satisfy. During Holy Week, when the rest of the Catholic world seems to put on a long face, Filipinos breathe the air of festivity, of community activity, in short, of a town *fiesta*. In their inimitable way they are able to transform the solemn Good Friday procession with the images of sorrow-striken saints into a religious fanfare.

The question that comes to mind at this point is whether the qualities of popular religiosity mentioned above are suited for the liturgy. Marsili points out that the form, style, and language of popular devotions do not have a direct bearing on their ability to acquire a "liturgical" character. The form, style, and language of the liturgy, he says, are matters that belong to the realm of cultural adaptation.[34] No single tradition can claim a monopoly over these elements. Some of the things inculturation affects are precisely the external aspects of the liturgy. It is not correct to determine whether the traits of popular religiosity are liturgically suited or not solely on the basis of comparison with the classical traits of the Roman liturgy.

The following consideration clarifies the point raised by Marsili. While the classical Roman liturgy manifests the qualities of brevity, sobriety, and directness, the Oriental liturgies often indulge in long-winded prayer formularies, colorful and dramatic rites, and repeated acts of venerating the icons. There are, in other words, other liturgi-

34. Marsili, "Liturgia e non-liturgia," 156.

cal traditions besides the Roman. Today, as the process of inculturation begins to gain ground in local Churches, the classical form of
the Roman liturgy is subjected to a type of modification comparable
to what transpired between the eighth and the tenth centuries, when
the Franco-Germanic people adapted the classical Roman Rite to
their local culture. From that time on, the *apologies,* which we can
describe as self-deprecatory prayers dearly loved by the Franco-
Germanic people, became a significant feature of the borrowed
Roman liturgy. A quick examination of these prayers is enough to assure us that both their structure and language are plainly of devotional extraction.

The conclusion is that it would not be accurate to make a judg-
ment, based exclusively on the classical Roman liturgy as the standard, on whether a given form, style, or language meets the
requirements of the liturgy. Historically and in actual practice, the
role played by the culture of local Churches in the formation of the
liturgy is by no means negligible. The bottom line is that the form,
style, and language of popular religiosity should not be regarded as
unsuitable for liturgical use merely because they show no affinity to
the classical Roman liturgy. In this connection Marsili's progressive
view is truly enlightening: "The authenticity of the liturgy cannot be
judged only by the standard of tradition or juridical sanction; the liturgy, provided its essential elements (to reveal the church and to ac-
tualize the mystery of Christ) are kept intact, can be expressed in
forms which the people of God, under the leadership of their pastors, consider more suited to their historical, cultural, and psychological situation."[35]

The process of inculturating the liturgy in the framework of popular religiosity implies reception on the part of the liturgy of the chief
features that characterize popular religiosity. These features are, to
borrow Valenziano's description, festive and dramatic, spontaneous
and creative, personal yet communitarian, otherworldly yet profoundly human, symbolic yet immediate.

Linguistic and Ritual Traits of Popular Religiosity. Since the liturgy
consists of formularies and gestures, it would be useful to take a

35. Ibid.

112

closer look at the kind of language and rites employed by various forms of popular religiosity.

A quick glance at the texts of novenas is enough to lead one to conclude that liturgists had nothing to do with them. Their language belongs to a totally different type of literary genre. While the Roman liturgical language is sober, direct, and linear, the language of the novena prayer texts is florid, discursive to the point of rambling, and vividly picturesque. Furthermore, while the Roman prayers tend to address the intellect, these normally appeal to the sentiments and emotions of people. Unlike the Roman form of petition, or the classic *ut* clause, which can be disarmingly straightforward, the petitionary form used in these texts is wrapped in words of self-deprecation, cajolement, and such conditional phrases as "if it so pleases you."[36]

It is not possible nor is it necessary to examine all the existing novenas in order to find out the type of literary genre they employ. But it would be an oversimplification to think that if one has seen a novena, one has seen all. Novenas are as varied as the people who create them, the saints to whom they are addressed, and the motives for which they are composed. However, there are certain traits that they share in common and that set them apart from the Roman euchological tradition. These traits, which we enumerated above, are easily visible in several of the forty-five novena prayers collected by Lovasik in his *Treasury of Novenas*.

The novena prayer to the Sacred Heart in this collection is a fine illustration of how popular devotions differ from the liturgical form of worship. Its rhetorical questions—a style totally unknown in the Roman euchological tradition—its words of cajolement, and its tone of familiarity, which is absolutely unthinkable in the liturgy, are typical of the particular literary genre of novenas. The text of this novena prayer merits closer examination than is possible here. Its rhetorical questions are meant to arouse in the heart of the devotee a sense of trust and security. "To whom can I turn if not to You, whose

36. For the characteristic traits of the Roman euchology, see T. Klauser, *A Short History of the Western Liturgy* (Oxford, 1979) 37–44; see also C. Mohrmann, *Liturgical Latin: Its Origin and Character* (Washington, 1957); S. Marsili, "Liturgical Texts for Modern Man," Concilium 2/5 (1969) 26–35; M. Augé, "Principi di interpretazione dei testi liturgici," Anamnesis 1 (Turin, 1974) 167–179.

Heart is the source of all graces and merits? Where should I seek if not in the treasure which contains all the riches of Your kindness and mercy? Where should I knock if not at the door through which God gives Himself to us and through which we go to God?"[37]

Boldness built upon personal intimacy and resolute faith underlies the following lines: "Dear Jesus, I firmly believe that You can grant me the grace I implore, even though it should require a miracle."[38] However, a spirit of deference and simplicity of heart, should the prayer not be granted, mark the following lines: "Sacred Heart, whatever may be Your decision with regard to my request, I will never stop adoring, loving, praising, and serving You."[39]

A literary trait we often observe in novena prayers is the discursive style they employ for catechetical or moral instruction. The long novena prayer to Our Lady of Lourdes in the same collection exemplifies this trait. A portion of the text reads: "Mary, Mother of God, I firmly believe in the doctrine of Holy Mother Church concerning your Immaculate Conception: namely, that you were, in the first instant of your conception, by the singular grace and privilege of God, in view of the merits of Jesus Christ, the Savior of the human race, preserved immune from the stain of original sin."[40]

The prayer becomes more discursive as it progresses: "By appearing in the Grotto of Lourdes, you were pleased to make it a privileged sanctuary, from which you dispense your favors; and already many sufferers have obtained the cure of their infirmities, both spiritual and corporal."[41]

The discursive style is not exclusive to novena prayers. Something of it is present also in some liturgical texts. Several prefaces, the collects for the Immaculate Conception and the Assumption, and the prayer after each reading at the Easter Vigil, though set in the framework of the Roman euchology, are unmistakably discursive and catechetical. The difference is that the liturgical formularies follow a

37. Lovasik, *Treasury of Novenas*, 111.
38. Ibid., 112.
39. Ibid.
40. Ibid., 158.
41. Ibid., 159.

well-defined structure and use a language marked by sobriety and due proportion.

Vivid and picturesque language is another literary trait we often meet in the texts of popular devotion. The novena prayer to Our Lady of Perpetual Help gives us a fine example of this particular trait: "We too have our crosses and trials. Sometimes they almost crush us to the ground."[42] Another example comes from the *Pasyon*, which is a Filipino masterpiece of popular religious poetry. The section containing the lamentations of the Blessed Virgin makes her exclaim, in an outpouring of motherly tenderness, as she gazes on the lifeless body of her son:

> Was not this the body that cast its shadow upon heaven and earth? Why has it dimmed and is now deprived of life?
>
> My Son, were not these the hands which you raised to bless all? Why are they pierced and bleeding?
>
> Was not this the hair I used to comb? Why is it unkempt and stained with blood?[43]

The text is reminiscent of the language of another Marian poem, the sequence *Stabat Mater*, also of devotional origin and character, which is now part of the Roman liturgy.

Popular religiosity is distinguished from the official worship of the Church not only in language but also in rite. Several forms of popular religiosity, especially devotions, use a set of devices to encourage active participation or at least a lively performance of the rite. Some of these are the communal recitation of every prayer if an assembly is present, repetitiveness, and litanic petitions. These ritual traits are, as a whole, not shared by the liturgy. Liturgical norms neatly define the role of each one in the hierarchical assembly, so that the recitation of certain formularies is strictly reserved to the president of the assembly. Furthermore, the liturgy, especially after the conciliar reform, avoids the repetition of the same prayer formularies. It would be very strange to hear the opening prayer repeated after the general

42. *Perpetual Help Novena* (Parañaque, Manila, 1973) 8.
43. *Kasaysayan ng Pasiong Mahal*, 171. Translation from Tagalog is mine.

intercessions, or to sing the Lord's Prayer twice during Mass. The liturgy has also reduced to the minimum the recitation of litanies or has shortened them, as in the baptismal liturgy.

In contrast to the liturgy, novenas often include the litanies proper to each, preferably the longer form, and almost invariably instruct the devotee to recite the Lord's Prayer, Hail Mary, and Glory Be at every turn. The repetition of familiar formularies often has a psychological effect: one gets the feeling and satisfaction of having personally said the prayers. Since popular devotions are by nature private and meant for individual recitation, they give little or no consideration to the role of the prayer leader, even when an assembly is present. The communal recitation of novenas always leaves one with the impression of having prayed in a personal way or even alone. This contrasts with liturgical practice. For example, the Liturgy of the Hours is often "celebrated" alone, yet it tenaciously maintains a choral form. The Mass, even with only one member of the faithful present, is likewise "celebrated," as if a large assembly were participating.

As regards ritual gestures, popular devotions generally connect the posture of kneeling with the prayer of petition. Kneeling at Mass is more reverential in purpose. That is why it is prescribed at the time of consecration. The general intercessions, which are petitionary in nature, are recited standing.[44] An exception exists. At the general intercessions on Good Friday, the people, at the direction of the conference of bishops, may kneel and pray silently for some time after each intention is announced, or they may either kneel or stand throughout the entire period of the intercessions.[45] The liturgy, like the novenas, also prescribes kneeling during the Litany of the Saints when it is recited outside Sunday and the Easter season.[46] It will be recalled that the Litany of the Saints was originally a popular responsorial prayer.

Popular devotions are expected to be performed in front of the

---

44. See *Institutio generalis Missalis Romani*, no. 21 (Vatican City, 1975); *DOL*, 474.

45. *Missale Romanum* (Vatican City, 1975) 251.

46. *Ordo professionis religiosae* (Vatican City, 1975) no. 66, p. 70; *De ordinatione episcopi, presbyterorum, et diaconorum* (Vatican City, 1990) no. 42, p. 15; *Missale Romanum*, no. 39, p. 281.

image of the saint being invoked. The novena to Our Lady of Perpetual Help instructs those unable to attend the devotion in church because of sickness to pray the novena at home before the picture of Our Lady of Perpetual Help.[47] It seems that sacred images are more than mere accessories of popular religiosity. The stations of the cross, which by definition imply movement from one station to another, can be made in a stationary manner for lack of space. But would there be stations of the cross without at least the crosses? Most processions would be unthinkable without images. The proliferation of sacred images in churches and homes is a sign of a vibrant devotional life of the faithful. They are not decorative artifacts: they are objects of devotion. And though our Western theology does not appropriate Saint John Damascene's teaching that sacred images are "channels" of divine grace in the manner of sacraments, the ordinary faithful who venerate sacred images regard them not as mere representations but as a presence, however vague the concept of "presence" may be, of the persons they represent.

Unlike popular religiosity, the Roman liturgy has little use for sacred images. In this connection SC 125 calls for the observance of restraint: "The practice of placing sacred images in churches so that they may be venerated by the faithful is to be maintained. Nevertheless there is to be restraint regarding their number and prominence so that they do not create confusion among the Christian people or foster religious practices of doubtful orthodoxy." The General Instruction of the Roman Missal gives to this conciliar norm the following interpretation: "There is need both to limit their number and to situate them in such a way that they do not distract the people's attention from the celebration. There is to be only one image of any one saint."[48] The *Rite of Dedication of a Church* adds that "in new churches statues and pictures of saints may not be placed above the altar."[49] In short, the number of sacred images in churches should be limited, they should not be exposed too prominently, and there should be only one image of any one saint. Except for the cross, which may be

47. *Perpetual Help Novena*, 2.
48. *Institutio generalis Missalis Romani*, no. 278; *DOL*, 521.
49. *Ordo dedicationis ecclesiae et altaris* (Vatican City, 1977), ch. 4, no. 10; *DOL*, 1380.

placed either on the altar or near it, the Roman liturgy appears to have little sympathy for sacred images.[50]

The impression given by these liturgical norms is that sacred images, apart from the danger of superstition they continually poise, detract the attention of the faithful from the celebration. Such an attitude of severity toward the use of sacred images is understandable in the light of the preconciliar exaggerations that considerably lessened the importance of the liturgy and active participation. Popular devotions regard sacred images in a different light. There is no competition between the images and devotional prayer. Rather, the presence of sacred images helps the devotees to fix their attention more firmly on what they pray. Sacred images do not distract; they enhance prayer and devotion. Obviously this consideration does not apply in places where popular religiosity is not part of the prayer life of the community. But in local Churches where popular religiosity is alive, it might be necessary to review the norms on the use of sacred images in the liturgy in order to foster a greater spirit of devotion and a more active participation in liturgical celebrations.

Popular religious drama like its medieval predecessors, of which some were definitely part of the liturgy, like the *peregrinus* play during the Divine Office in monasteries, is strongly mimetic in expression. The script of the medieval *peregrinus*, for example, directs the performers "to walk about looking sad" as the Emmaus gospel is narrated. The play *hortulanus*, which dramatizes the meeting of the risen Christ and Mary Magdalene, instructs the person who plays the role of Mary "to walk slowly as if in search of something, in imitation of Mary Magdalene."[51] The importance of mimesis or imitativeness is particularly heightened in the way religious drama is presented. The *cenaculo* and *encuentro* are dramatic reenactments through realistic imitation. Even the statues of the risen Christ and the Blessed Virgin are made to bow to each other at the *encuentro* as a sign of Easter greeting. In some places the head of the statue of Christ crucified is, by some mechanism, made to bow when John 19:30 is read at the proclamation of the Passion on Good Friday. Religious drama is not

50. *Institutio generalis Missalis Romani*, no. 270; *DOL*, 519.
51. A. Chupungco, "Anàmnesis and Mimesis in the Celebration of Easter Sunday," *Studia anselmiana* 102 (Rome, 1990) 263–268.

118

only mimetic, it is also realistic, sometimes to the point of, alas, becoming gross. It is clear that popular religiosity has no use for abstract forms.

The Roman liturgy, of course, is not entirely lacking in drama and mimesis. The rubric for the narration of the institution at Mass directs the priest to take the bread and the chalice as he recites the words "he took bread" and "he took the cup." At the words "looking up to heaven" of the Roman Canon the priest is instructed to look upwards. The Palm Sunday procession and the washing of feet on Holy Thursday are other obvious examples of mimesis in the Roman liturgy. To this list we may add the proclamation of the Passion, which is a dramatic type of reading. Surely drama and mimesis are not original to the Roman liturgy. What comes across through these random examples is that the classical form of the Roman liturgy has not been insensitive to popular expressions.

From the data we have so far examined, we were able to identify the principal features of popular religiosity. These are, first, their literary genre, which is marked by discursive and picturesque quality; second, their use of sacred images; third, their preference for such devices for participation as repetitiveness and communal recitation; and fourth, their use of dramatic forms that are often strongly mimetic or imitative.

The task of the liturgist is to study how such traits can influence the shape of the Roman liturgy in those local Churches where popular religiosity thrives vigorously. It is to be taken for granted that not every element of popular religiosity is liturgically suitable or even capable of expressing the nature and purpose of the liturgy. It is likewise evident that we may not, in the name of adaptation or inculturation, transform the liturgy into a form of popular religiosity. But neither may we continue to ignore the gap that exists between the official worship *of* the Church and the popular worship *in* the Church. The difference between the two must always exist, and inculturation must not eradicate it lest an irreparable imbalance in the prayer life of the Church be created. But the gap between them has to be bridged, in order to make the liturgy more accessible to people and popular religiosity richer in doctrine and spirituality, or, in the words of the *Document of Puebla*, in order to bring about "a mutual and enriching exchange between the liturgy and popular devotion."

One important principle of inculturation is that it must neither debilitate nor damage the identity of any of the parties involved. Inculturation means mutual enrichment, not destruction. It operates according to the principle of transculturation. In the process of interaction and mutual assimilation the parties evolve and undergo transformation without entering thereby into a crisis of identity.[52] It will be recalled that the formula for inculturation, which we discussed in the first chapter of this work, namely $A+B = C$, means that, thanks to the process of mutual assimilation, A and B evolve into C, but on account of the principle of transculturation, A and B retain their identity.

In other words, we should be careful not to reduce the liturgy in the name of inculturation to a form of popular religiosity or, in reverse, to convert the exercise of popular religiosity to a liturgical action. Above all we should be wary about suppressing popular devotions in the name of liturgical renewal, as if they posed a threat to the integrity of worship. In this connection, Pope Paul VI strongly criticized "the attitude of some engaged in the pastoral ministry who, rejecting popular devotions *a priori*, suppress them (whereas in fact, when rightly conducted, they are endorsed by the magisterium). Such people thus create a vacuum they cannot fill. Clearly they forget that the Council did not direct the elimination of popular devotions but rather their harmonization with the liturgy."[53]

A certain leeway should nevertheless be given to the affirmation made by Marsili that in particular instances the authority of the Church can declare that some of the existing popular devotions— even in their present popular form and style—are liturgical celebrations.[54] According to him there is no such thing as a single standard shape of the liturgy. Though the liturgical reform of Vatican II opted for the classical shape, it did not close the door to other possible shapes. This is in fact what articles 37–40 of the Constitution on the Liturgy are all about. Hence, the fact that the language and ritual elements of popular religiosity are alien to the character of the classi-

52. Idem: *Liturgies of the Future: The Process and Methods of Inculturation* (New York, 1989) 31.
53. Paul VI, *Marialis cultus*, no. 31; DOL, 1220.
54. Marsili, "Liturgia e non-liturgia," 156.

cal Roman liturgy is not a premise for excluding them from the ambit of the liturgy. The question of what is liturgical and what is not rests ultimately on the authority of the Church.

At this point it might be useful to note that the view held by Marsili actually transcends the confines of inculturation. He does not in reality address the issue of of introducing pertinent and suitable features of popular religiosity into the liturgy. He does not, in other words, deal with inculturation. Rather, on the basis of historical facts, he speaks of the power of Church authority to declare that a given form of popular religiosity like the rosary or a procession, even without previously subjecting them to a liturgical transformation, is to be considered a liturgical rite, that is, included among the official celebrations *of* the Church. In the context of the present study we would not call such a process "inculturation" but "aggregation."

The Method of Dynamic Equivalence. Inculturation, as we have seen early on, means that by the principle of transculturation the forms of popular religiosity are not raised to the status and dignity of liturgy and the liturgy does not become merely another form of popular religiosity. A method that can ensure the observance of transculturation is dynamic equivalence. We have seen that this method consists basically in replacing the structure, language, and rite of the Roman liturgy with cultural elements that have an equal meaning or value and are able to transmit the message intended by the Roman liturgy. Applying this to the subject at hand, we may regard the forms and characteristic features of popular religiosity as the cultural elements that enter into the dynamic of interaction with the liturgy. What the method of dynamic equivalence aims to achieve is to make the Roman liturgy shed its classical shape and put on the qualities and forms of expression typical of popular religiosity.

Dynamic equivalence is not a question of introducing the forms of popular religiosity such as devotions, processions, drama, and dance into the liturgical celebration through the method of acculturation, though we should not exclude this method a priori. Acculturation is, after all, a valid approach to the question, even if it has the limitations we have pointed out earlier. Nor is the method of raising certain forms of popular religiosity to the status of a liturgical rite through aggregation to be excluded. Dynamic equivalence, which neither acculturation nor aggregation employs as a method, operates through the assimilation of the characteristic traits, not the forms, of popular religiosity.

The liturgy resulting from the use of dynamic equivalence will not necessarily please the historians of the Roman liturgy who hold a special predilection for things that are classical, but it will assuredly have a popular appeal. We may characterize such a liturgy, to borrow Valenziano's description of popular religiosity, as "festive, felt, spontaneous; expressive, immediate, human; communitarian, collective, joyful, symbolic, traditional, alive." We could probably name it "popular liturgy," in contrast to "classical liturgy," because its pattern of thought, language, and ritualization will not be any different from the pattern we observe in popular religiosity. Its language will not have the measured, hieratic, and sober character of classical liturgy. It will be marked by human warmth and touch, colorful expressions, and elaborate embellishments. Its ritual gestures will be regulated not by the standard norms of the classical Roman liturgy but by the living traditions of popular religiosity.

It is hoped that the prospect of a popular type of liturgy will not cause dismay among postconciliar liturgical reformers. Should a popular liturgy ever become a reality in those local Churches where popular religiosity is an integral part of Christian life of worship, it would not, of course, be the first time. The Franco-Germanic liturgy of the eighth century was profoundly influenced by elements of popular religiosity. The *apologies*, which have crept into the Roman liturgy, are an uncontested proof of this.

But would a popular liturgy still be the liturgy of the Roman Church? The question is by no means easy to answer. If we consider the classical form or, at any rate, the form presented by the typical editions of the liturgical books an essential element of the Roman liturgy, the answer is quite obvious. But is the classical form essential to the Roman liturgy of Vatican II or at least to the family of the Roman liturgy? Marsili, whose reflection on the topic we had the occasion to cite early on, does not think so. In fact, historians of liturgy regard the Franco-Germanic of the eighth century as a type of the Roman liturgy, not pure and classical to be sure, but Roman nonetheless. The name they affix to the tenth-century *Romano-Germanic Pon-*

tifical is evidence of their thinking. Furthermore, the shape of the medieval liturgy codified by the Tridentine reformers could not be further removed from the classical form of the Roman Rite. Lastly, the Vatican II typical editions themselves contain a section on norms for adapting the Roman liturgy to the culture and traditions of various peoples. We know that cultural adaptation, or inculturation, necessarily modifies the classical shape of the liturgy.

We conclude from these considerations that historically and in actual legislation the concept of Roman liturgy does not include the classical form as one of its integral and, much less, essential elements. Hence, the popular qualities inspired by popular religiosity do not necessarily detract from the official status of a liturgical rite. What appears to be the qualifying condition, so that a particular form of worship can be considered Roman liturgy, is adherence to the doctrinal and spiritual content presented by the typical editions of the liturgical books. Fidelity to the content is the principal consideration here, and the method of dynamic equivalence offers precisely the assurance that the content is faithfully preserved and transmitted in the process of change. What is modified is the shape, the pattern of thought and language, the cultural expression. Inculturation is a type of dynamic translation: it does not change the content, it reexpresses it.

It would be useful to clarify at this point what dynamic equivalence is and what it is not in relation to popular religiosity. Dynamic equivalence does not mean combining or merging with liturgical celebrations such forms of popular religiosity as processions, rosary, and novenas, which would result in a corresponding loss of their identity. Dynamic equivalence is not the same as Marsili's concept of aggregation, whereby certain forms of popular devotion are raised to the rank of liturgical rites. Neither is it an assimilation in whole or in part of popular devotions. Some have badly read *SC* 13 and badly applied it by combining Mass and popular devotions like novenas and the rosary into a hybrid celebration. Pope Paul VI rightly sounded the alarm when he warned that such a practice could result in turning the memorial of the paschal mystery into a simple setting for some popular devotion: "We wish to remind those acting in this way of the conciliar norm: popular devotions must be subordinated to the liturgy, not intermingled with it."[55] In places where this was done the inspiration was taken from the practice of integrating the Divine Office with the Mass. This meant that the litany and the novena prayer took the place of the general intercessions, while the novena songs were distributed to the different parts of the Mass.

Dynamic equivalence has nothing to do with such methods of "inculturation." It operates in an altogether different manner. It analyzes the forms and characteristic traits of popular religiosity, identifying those elements that can influence the shape of a liturgical rite. This means that the various forms of popular religiosity like novenas and processions or their linguistic and ritual traits are not inserted into the liturgical rite, thereby becoming part of it. Physical incorporation (the expression is redundant) and inspiration are two different modes of assimilation. Dynamic equivalence is more at ease with the latter. The weight of popular religiosity on the liturgy is felt more as an inspiration than as an imposition.

The aim to be achieved through dynamic equivalence is to give a popular expression to the liturgical texts, rites, and symbols by taking inspiration from popular religiosity. The formularies of the liturgy are not transposed into novena prayers. They conserve their euchological character, namely the elements of anamnesis and epiclesis, or petition. Prefaces retain their basic structure, consisting of an exordium, embolism, and concluding formula.[56] Furthermore, their doctrinal content, which is presented by the Roman Sacramentary, is preserved. But dynamic equivalence changes the literary genre of these formularies from classical to popular. They cease to employ the classical rhetorical figures of antithesis, parallelism, redundancy, rhyme, and cursus. Their literary genre assimilates the discursive, florid, picturesque, and repetitive qualities of popular religious literature.

Through dynamic equivalence, the ritual aspect of the liturgy also undergoes a transformation. Obviously the different movements and the posture of standing, kneeling, or sitting continue to signify the community and the unity of the assembly and to express and foster

55. Paul VI, *Marialis cultus*, no. 31; *DOL*, 1220; see Castellano, "Religiosidad popular y liturgia," 1739–1741.
56. See M. Augé: "Principi di interpretazione dei testi liturgici," Anamnesis 1 (Casale Monferrato, 1988) 171–178.

the spiritual attitude of those taking part in the liturgical celebration.[57] Likewise the offertory and Communion processions retain both their functional and symbolic character. They do not become an exercise of Eucharistic devotion. The dramatic and mimetic parts of the celebration also continue to narrate in a graphic manner the saving events. But they do not become an occasion for costumed performers to indulge in theatrical display. The point is that some of the ritual qualities of popular religiosity can, through the prudent use of dynamic equivalence, relieve some of our liturgical celebrations of rubrical rigidity and temper it with an amount of spontaneity, vivacity, color, and human warmth.

Inculturation should be the normal process for inserting popular religious expressions into the liturgy, and dynamic equivalence the suitable method to ensure that the content of the liturgy is duly safeguarded. Nevertheless, dynamic equivalence is not officially the exclusive method of inculturation. In 1971 the Congregation for Divine Worship allowed for the Philippines a practice that has apparently no precedent in recent history. It allowed the *encuentro* to take the place of the entrance rite of the Mass at Easter dawn.[58] The *encuentro* is both drama and procession with a well-defined ritual shape. Unlike the procession on Palm Sunday, it does not possess anything that can qualify it as liturgical, except for the antiphon *Regina coeli* sung by the "angel." Unlike the medieval dramas, it does not employ the liturgical ministers as performers, nor is it held in church in the course of a liturgical celebration. But it is a procession similar to Palm Sunday, and it is, strictly speaking, not a popular devotion but drama. These are some considerations that justify its being integrated with the celebration of the Mass.

From a methodological point of view, this method of combining the *encuentro* with the Mass, though the result is a significant breakthrough in the strained relationship between liturgy and popular religiosity, falls short of the requirements of inculturation. What we find here is not inculturation but acculturation, or a juxtaposition of a liturgical rite and a form of popular religiosity. Unlike inculturation,

57. See *Institutio generalis Missalis Romani*, no. 20; DOL, 474.
58. See *The Liturgical Information Bulletin of the Philippines* 6 (March–April 1971) 32–33.

acculturation does not encourage mutual assimilation. While the Palm Sunday procession is now fully integrated with the liturgy of the Mass, the *encuentro* remains a charming little drama at some point in the Easter dawn procession before the celebration of the Mass. But it is very much a foreign element in the Roman Mass, which has nothing to say about the supposed meeting between the risen Christ and his mother. Nonetheless, popular religiosity must satisfy the human sentiment of piety by dramatizing a meeting that filial devotion alone has been able to record.

Popular Religiosity and the Liturgical Texts. In practice, how does dynamic equivalence operate? Studies made on the Christmas collect *Deus, qui humanae substantiae dignitatem,* attributed to Pope Leo I, inform us of its elaborate rhetorical features as well as its sublime theological content, which focuses on human dignity against the contrary claims of Manicheans.[59] But as a formulary the collect is devoid of human sentiments and imagery. In fact, its protasis does not even allude to the birth of Christ, while its apodosis, for all its theological wealth, barely suggests that we are celebrating Christmas. Yet in this collect we find the necessary premises for a possible interaction between liturgical texts and the language of popular religiosity. The rhetorical figures of vivacity, redundancy, repetition, and sound give to the collect a classic literary elegance. And it is these rhetorical figures that open the door to dynamic equivalence, to the possibility of substituting them with the literary genre proper to popular religiosity. In other words, the vivacity of this Latin collect readily gives way to the picturesque language employed by popular religiosity—its redundancy gives way to discursiveness; its repetition to repetitiveness; and its sound to floridity. The literary qualities of the Leonine formulary are not totally lost; rather they are dynamically translated.

As regards content, scholars tell us that the Latin text brings into focus our human nature, on which God conferred a new dignity through the incarnation of Jesus Christ. Human dignity is the key idea of this formulary, as it was also the pervading thought in several

59. See the study of A. Echiegu, *Translating the Collects of the "Sollemnitates Domini" of the "Missale Romanum" of Paul VI in the Language of the African* (Münster, 1984) 122–227.

of Pope Leo I's homilies. Christmas, according to this collect, was the moment when God restored to us our dignity by sending Christ into our world in order to become one of us. This doctrine is not absent from popular thinking, but it is expressed in another way. In popular religiosity Christmas means the crib in which the Son of God was laid. However richly the crib is adorned, it is always the symbol of human poverty and unworthiness, which God deigned to visit and uplift. It may appear strange, but the dynamic equivalent of human dignity in popular religiosity is the Christmas crib. Consequently, some allusion, even if only a glancing one, to the crib and to what it symbolizes will not only enrich the collect with a picturesque and traditional quality but in the final analysis will also translate the Latin text more faithfully.

To get a clearer picture of the meeting point between liturgy and popular religiosity, it might be useful to exhibit here the Leonine collect and a representative text from a collection of popular religious formularies for Christmas. Normally the original Latin collect should be the liturgical *terminus a quo*, but for purposes of textual comparison the 1974 English translation of the collect will do. When reading the two texts one should keep in mind the particular literary genre of each text and make a mental note of how the popular religious formulary could influence the content and literary expression of the collect.

The English collect, which badly needs revision for its exclusive language, reads:

> Lord God,
> we praise you for creating man,
> and still more for restoring him in Christ.
> Your Son shared our weakness:
> may we share his glory.[60]

The other *terminus a quo*, a novena prayer for Christmas, is made of several paragraphs. The pertinent portions read:

In Your crib I see the most wondrous love that ever was—the

60. *The Sacramentary* (New York, 1974) 44.

love of God humbling Himself so low to beg the love of our hearts. Give me the grace to love You in return with a deep, true, personal love.

May I come eagerly and often to unite myself closely to You in Your Sacrament of Love. The church shall be my Bethlehem; the altar, the crib; the sacred species of bread and wine, the swaddling clothes by which I can recognize You as my God, and under which I can, as Mary and Joseph and the shepherds did, take You into my arms; yes, even receive You into my heart—a grace which even the Angels envy me.

Jesus, from the crib You teach the world the true dignity of humility. Poverty, suffering, and humiliation stand by Your cross and by Your crib.[61]

It is not necessary to enter into the mechanics of how the literary genre and content of the above novena prayer can inject vivacity and color into the liturgical formulary. We have, on several occasions, addressed this particular question. What might be opportune to point out here is the extensive use of allegory in the novena prayer. Although the medieval liturgy was not unfamiliar with this type of interpretation, the Church has often shown a reticent attitude toward it. Allegorical interpretation, which flourished in the school of Alexandria during the patristic period, aroused great sympathy among ordinary people during the Middle Ages. Surprisingly, it is sparingly employed by popular religiosity. In fact, popular religiosity tends to read biblical narratives rather literally, as we can observe in its dramas and representations.

The method of dynamic equivalence can be applied when dealing with almost any liturgical formulary. For instance, the prayer of the faithful, or general intercessions, has all the ingredients necessary for interaction with popular religiosity. On the whole, its basic elements are shared also by the prayers of petitions found in devotional prayer books. According to the postconciliar Concilium, the prayer of the faithful has the following characteristics: "It is a petition addressed to God; it is a petition to God chiefly for blessings of a universal kind;

61. Lovasik, *Treasury of Novenas*, 34.

it belongs to the whole congregation."[62] Because it is structured, formal, and direct, it differs from the devotional type of petitions, which are generally discursive, conditional, and personal.

In the process of inculturation certain elements of the prayer of the faithful must, of course, be preserved. Roman tradition requires that it be addressed to God the Father through Christ. The prayer embraces the general needs of the Church, the nation, the world, and the community. It is not a private prayer but a public form of petitions, even if the people, as on Good Friday, remain silent except when they respond Amen. Apart from these conditions, there is no limit to how popular religiosity can influence the shape of the prayer of the faithful. The straightforward petitions of the Roman formularies, which may seem to some cultural groups to contain a note of discourtesy because of the frequent use of the imperative form, can be couched in some deferential phraseology typical of novena prayers. The attitude of deference and respect is exemplified by the novena prayer to the Immaculate Heart of Mary: "Dearest Mother, if what I ask for should not be according to God's Will, pray that I may receive that which will be of greater benefit to my soul."[63]

We are not suggesting that the prayer of the faithful should normally consist of conditional sentences, but something of a deferential attitude should not be totally absent from it either. Obviously, what the Church prays for during the liturgy will never be contrary to God's will, but popular religiosity always prudently leaves some margin for its realization. It expresses openly what the liturgy only implies: God is free to do as God pleases, and we should be ready to accept what God wills. This sentiment seems to be the underlying reason for the use of conditional clauses in novena prayers.

Popular religiosity can also influence and modify the element of directness that often characterizes the prayer of the faithful. Strict pertinence and sparing use of words have a peculiar effect on the Roman formularies: they sound like a list of shopping items. There is a notable exception to this, namely the series of general intercessions on Good Friday. Apart from this, the sample texts for the prayer of

62. Concilium, "The Universal Prayer or Prayer of the Faithful," no. 2; DOL, 595.
63. Lovasik, *Treasury of Novenas*, 164.

the faithful proposed by the *Roman Missal* are a genuine specimen of the *sobrietas romana*.

> For the holy Church of God:
> that the Lord guide and protect it,
> we pray to the Lord.

> For all the peoples of the world:
> that the Lord unite them in peace and harmony,
> we pray to the Lord.

> For all our brothers and sisters in need:
> that the Lord assist them,
> we pray to the Lord.[64]

The antithesis of *sobrietas romana* is a long-windedness typical of the formularies employed for popular devotions. The following portions of the petitions addressed to the Immaculate Heart of Mary are random samples of what may be called "conversational discursiveness," which some Roman liturgists will probably describe as nothing more than a desultory or rambling loquacity.

> Mary, I admire that deep humility which troubled your blessed Heart at the message of the Angel Gabriel when he announced that you had been chosen to be the Mother of the Son of the most high God. You considered yourself only God's lowly handmaid. Ashamed at the sight of my own pride, I beg you the grace of a contrite and humble heart so that I may acknowledge my misery and reach the glory promised to the truly humble of heart.

> Blessed Virgin, you kept in your Heart the precious treasure of the words of Jesus your Son and, pondering over the sublime mysteries they contained, you lived only for God. How ashamed I am of my coldness of heart! Dear Mother, obtain for me the grace of meditating always on the holy law of God and

---

64. *The Sacramentary*, 992.

of seeking to follow your example in fervent practice of all the Christian virtues.[65]

This type of petition obviously belongs to a literary genre that is absolutely alien to the classical Roman form of intercessory prayer. However, as we remarked early on, the classical form is not the only possible liturgical form. It would be difficult to bring forward any valid objection based on liturgical tradition to a type of the prayer of the faithful whose structure and language have been inspired by popular religiosity. We should, of course, be wary of the kind of discursiveness in prayer that becomes preachy or homiletic. But this is a danger we can observe in lengthy liturgical prayers that have been composed, even without the direct influence of popular religiosity, for the immediate purpose of instruction or edification rather than adoration.

Popular Religiosity and the Liturgical Rites. Not only the liturgical texts but also gestures and symbols can acquire, through dynamic equivalence, a popular character. The liturgy has never acknowledged the existence of the Christmas crib and the lantern signifying the star of Bethlehem. While Easter liturgy has its paschal candle and baptismal font, the Christmas liturgy is unusually devoid of symbols and images. But in reality, what Church does not have a Christmas crib? In many parts of the world the crib appears to be the pivotal element of the midnight Mass, and the solemn ceremony of laying the infant in the manger, the high point of the celebration. During the Easter season the liturgy pays particular attention to the paschal candle, which symbolizes the light of the risen Christ. Indeed, the Easter *Exsultet* is a *laus cerei*. In contrast, popular religiosity has introduced its own counterpart, the statue of the risen Christ holding the white banner of victory and raising the right hand to impart the blessing of peace. In places where popular religiosity thrives, what image could have a more immediate appeal to the people than this one? Surely the paschal candle is a rich liturgical symbol, but candle and realistic representation speak differently to people.

Are there concrete points of dialogue between popular religiosity

65. Lovasik, *Treasury of Novenas*, 165.

and the liturgy? Popular religiosity has a set of ritual gestures, which it borrowed from the liturgy but to which it has assigned in several instances another or an opposite meaning. For example, in popular religious usage, kneeling, not standing, is the appropriate posture for the prayer of petition. Touching and kissing sacred images are signs not so much of veneration as of communion with the person the image represents. Bowed head, a gesture that in the liturgy expresses prayer for God's blessing, signifies contrition. The sign of the cross is made not only to begin and end an activity but also to acknowledge the presence of God and his saints. That is why there are people who sign themselves with the cross when the consecrated bread and wine are raised, or when they pass a church or the image of a saint. Sometimes the sign of the cross is also used to ward off evil and beg divine assistance in time of trial and misfortune. Religious dances express joy, petition, and thanksgiving. Religious dramas are mimetic, because they are meant to be graphic forms of catechesis. Processions are a public proclamation of faith, and the sacred images are a reminder that another sphere of life exists beyond the present one.

To foster a more popular style of participation in the liturgy, certain acclamations and responses could be given a litanic structure or format without thereby suggesting that litanies should be incorporated into every liturgical celebration. A number of liturgical rites, like baptism, ordination, and religious profession, already include the Litany of the Saints. To stress the catechetical aspect of the liturgy in the manner and style of popular religiosity, the rubrics could encourage dramatic and mimetic performance of certain parts of the liturgy. This would be particularly appropriate to those occasions when the liturgy takes on a narrational form.[66] And to inspire a deeper Eucharistic devotion, the recitation of the Eucharistic Prayer could be accompanied by fitting gestures and symbols derived from popular expressions of devotion to the Blessed Sacrament. Though some forms of Eucharistic devotion had an unwholesome effect on the centrality of the Mass during the baroque period, in their own way they nurtured the people's love for the Eucharist.

66. See *Heiliger Dienst* 1/2 (1990), especially the contributions of P. Schmidkonz, "Die Dramaturgie der Liturgie in der Praxis der Gemeindemesse," 21–37; and H. Meyer, "Liturgie als (Kult-) Drama," 59–71.

It might be useful to reexamine in the light of popular religiosity the sparing and reticent use of banners and sacred images in liturgical celebrations. They are so much part and parcel of the people's act of worship that their absence from the liturgy can create a feeling of void that the formularies, however graphic and embellished, will not be able to fill. A careful study, perhaps a sociological research, should be made on the role sacred images have in creating the kind of religious setting needed for worship. Do sacred images—the number has in fact relative value—distract the worshipers from the liturgical mystery, or does their absence detract the sense of devotion and festivity from the celebration?[67]

These are random examples of how popular religiosity can influence the structure, language, gestures, and symbols of liturgical rites. Since we are dealing with the method of dynamic equivalence, the examples have necessarily been confined to what this method represents. Throughout this discussion we paid careful attention to the way dynamic equivalence operates, in order not to run the risk of what Pope Paul VI has described as the intermingling of popular devotion with the liturgy. The examples given above tell us the kind of toilsome effort required by dynamic equivalence. Any other method would be simpler. However, the method of dynamic equivalence ensures us that both liturgy and popular religiosity are able to keep their identity intact and integral throughout the process of interaction and mutual assimilation.

There is no better way to conclude this chapter than by reproducing again the text of the *Document of Puebla*: "We should encourage a mutual and enriching exchange between the liturgy and popular devotion, so that the yearning expressed in prayer and charisms, which is present in our countries today, may be channeled with clarity and prudence. On the other hand, popular religiosity, with its wealth of symbols and expressions, can share its creative dynamism with the liturgy. With due discernment such a dynamism can help to incarnate better in our culture the universal prayer of the church."[68]

---

67. See, however, *SC* 125 and the *Institutio generalis Missalis Romani*, no. 278; *DOL*, 521.

68. *Documento de Puebla*, "La evangelización en el presente y en el futuro de América Latina," no. 465, p. 167.

Chapter Four

The Inculturation of Liturgical Catechesis

Liturgical renewal, which can rightly be considered the hallmark of
Vatican II, is the confluence of several factors, namely the revision of
the typical editions of liturgical books, the translation and adaptation
of these to local situations, the rediscovery of the theological and
spiritual dimensions of liturgical rites, the active role of laypersons as
liturgical ministers, and the renewed interest in liturgical catechesis.
Among these factors liturgical catechesis deserves more than the
scant attention it is receiving at the present time from liturgists and
pastors. It is, after all, the mainstay of liturgical renewal.

It is not an exaggeration to say that without catechesis Vatican II's
program of reform would not have gotten off the ground in the first
place. The liturgical rites would surely have claimed the people's attention because of their novelty, but in the absence of catechesis their
initial interest would have abated before long. To many they would
have appeared as new gimmicks to bring the people back to church.
Without catechesis, the postconciliar program of liturgical inculturation, which is ahead of every local Church, cannot move forward.
Changes in the liturgical texts and rites, even if they reflect the living
culture and traditions of a local Church, always require explanation.
The relationship between liturgy and culture is not always evident.
Though *SC* 34 exhorts that the rites should, as a rule, not require
much explanation, the people still need to be enlightened on several
aspects, both spiritual and cultural, of the liturgical celebration. In
other words, catechesis is an indispensable companion of liturgical
renewal.

Papal Teaching on Liturgy and Catechesis. In the apostolic exhortation *Evangelii nuntiandi* Pope Paul VI addressed the problems that

134

threatened to thwart the effectivity of catechesis.[1] He admits with concern: "We are well aware that today's people seem to be sated with talk, often tired of listening, and, what is worse, to be hardening themselves against words. We are also aware that many psychologists and sociologists express the view that our contemporaries have passed beyond a culture of the word, which is now ineffective and useless, and now live in the culture of the image." If this view is correct, catechesis, too, must shift from a culture of word to a culture of image. In the thinking of the Pope, the shift involves the employment of "the modern resources this civilization has produced."

Modernization is surely a step to be taken if catechesis is to be renewed or updated, but it is only the first of so many others. People harden themselves against words not only because words often lack the power to evoke images from life but also because the message they communicate is not relevant, that is, not related to their cultural life and traditions. In the area of liturgical catechesis, the message, which is furnished by the liturgical texts and rites, often does not leave any lasting impression because it has no significant bearing on the concrete life of the listeners.

Four years before the publication of *Evangelii nuntiandi* the Vatican Congregation for the Clergy issued the *General Catechetical Directory*, which outlines the role of catechesis in liturgical renewal.[2] According to this document one of the chief forms the ministry of the word takes is catechesis. To catechesis the *Directory* assigns the task of fostering active, conscious, and genuine participation in liturgical celebrations, "not merely by explaining the meaning of the ceremonies, but also by forming the minds of the faithful for prayer, for thanksgiving, for repentance, for prayer with confidence, for a community spirit, and for understanding correctly the meaning of the creeds." Thus, catechesis is at the service of Vatican II's liturgical renewal, especially of sacramental life. In regard to this the *Directory* exhorts catechists to present the sacraments as sacraments of faith, which require proper dispositions, and as sources of grace for individuals and

1. Pope Paul VI, *Evangelii nuntiandi,* no. 42. English text in *Documents on the Liturgy,* 1963–1979 (Collegeville, 1982) 589. Henceforth *DOL.*
2. Congregation for the Clergy, *Directorium catechisticum generale, AAS* 64 (1972) 97–176. English excerpts in *DOL,* 359–368.

communities. Moreover, catechists should place much importance on the explanation of sacramental signs, since "catechesis should lead the faithful through the visible signs to ponder God's invisible mysteries of salvation."[3]

The connection between the proclamation of the word and sacramental celebration, or between the word of God and the sacrament, appears to be the theological ground for linking catechesis with the liturgy. Catechesis, which is a form of preaching the word of God, leads to the celebration of the sacraments by shedding light on their meaning and purpose and by instilling in the faithful the required dispositions. Pope Paul VI echoes this in *Evangelii nuntiandi*, no. 47, saying that evangelization, of which catechesis is an essential element, unfolds all its richness when it shows the close connection between the word and the sacraments. However, the celebration of the sacraments without the solid support of catechesis will in great measure deprive the sacraments of their efficacy. "The task of evangelization," the Pope concludes, "is precisely to educate Christians in the faith, so that they may live the sacraments as true sacraments of faith and not receive them in a passive manner."

Besides the need for a modern and relevant approach to catechesis, there is another need that is probably as urgent. Pastors and catechists have to be more keenly aware that catechesis cannot be treated in isolation from its source and summit, namely the liturgical celebration. In the apostolic exhortation *Catechesi tradendae* Pope John Paul II offers a clear insight on the nature of catechesis and its rapport with the liturgy. He writes in no uncertain terms that "catechesis is intrinsically linked with the whole of liturgical and sacramental activity, for it is in the sacraments, especially in the Eucharist, that Christ Jesus works in fullness for the transformation of human beings."

If the aim of catechesis is to give growth to the seed of faith sown with the initial proclamation of the gospel and effectively transmitted by the sacraments of initiation, it follows that catechesis has to operate within the framework of the liturgy. The Pope strongly stresses this point when he affirms that "catechesis always has reference to

3. Ibid., no. 57; *DOL*, 361–362.

the sacraments."[4] He concludes that "the catechesis that prepares for the sacraments is an eminent kind, and every form of catechesis necessarily leads to the sacraments of faith." The Pope is obviously echoing here the teaching of the Constitution on the Liturgy, articles 9–11, about the need for proper disposition on the part of the faithful and the full awareness of what they do when they participate in the celebration of the liturgy. The Constitution assigns to catechesis this particular role of preparing the faithful for the liturgy.

Nevertheless, "authentic practice of the sacraments is bound to have a catechetical aspect." With these words the Pope alludes to article 33 of the same constitution, which underlines the catechetical dimension of the liturgy: "Although the liturgy is above all things the worship of the divine majesty, it likewise contains rich instruction for the faithful." The Pope points out that "sacramental life is impoverished and very soon turns into hollow ritualism if it is not based on serious knowledge of the meaning of the sacraments, and catechesis becomes intellectualized if it fails to come alive in the sacramental practice."[5] Thus, liturgical catechesis should draw its material from the liturgical, particularly the sacramental, celebrations of the Church.

Catechesis from a Liturgical Perspective. Catechesis as an apostolic endeavor of the Church finds in the liturgy its summit and fount, to use the expression of article 10 of the Constitution on the Liturgy. It is not enough for catechists to propose and explain dogmatic statements and moral principles; it is necessary that they elucidate as well how the Church lives its faith when it celebrates the liturgy. The word of God, the euchological texts, and the various symbols used in the liturgy offer to catechists eminent and truly valuable material for instruction. In fact, the liturgy, whose rites are an experiential evocation of faith, interprets and proclaims the faith the Church received from the apostles. For this reason, catechesis not only leads to the sacraments of faith, it also draws its didactic elements from the liturgy, which, according to *SC* 33, "contains rich instruction for the faithful." But here it is necessary to add a caution: Though the liturgy

---

4. John Paul II, *Catechesi tradendae*, no. 23. English text in *Going, Teach . . .* (Boston, 1980), 644. Henceforth *GT.*
5. Ibid., 644–645.

has a strong educational dimension, it is celebrated not for the advantages it offers to catechesis but for its own end, namely the worship of God by the Church through Christ in the Spirit. "The liturgy," says *SC* 33, "is above all things the worship of the divine majesty."

The foregoing reflections on how catechesis relates to the liturgy are skillfully summed up by D. Sartore under three headings.[6] First of all, catechesis is an initiation into the liturgy. In the framework of salvation history and the life of the Church and with the aid of the modern human sciences, catechesis reveals to the faithful the hidden meaning of liturgical actions. Catechesis initiates the faithful into the world of sacramental symbolism, made up of things, actions, and words that lead them to a fruitful participation in the saving mystery of Christ. Though Sartore does not explicitly say so, it is obvious that the underlying theological consideration here is the binomial principle of word and sacrament, a principle that assigns to the sacraments a place of primacy in the economy of salvation. The word of God leads to the celebration of the sacraments by imparting faith and strengthening it in those who already believe. Catechesis shares the function of the word by preparing the faithful for the celebration of the sacraments.

Furthermore, liturgical celebrations are "catechesis in action." The expression comes from the *Directory on the Renewal of Catechesis*, published by the Italian conference of bishops in 1970. The very shape of the liturgy, consisting of the word of God and symbols corresponding to the nature of human psychology, makes it a unique form of catechesis. Sartore is careful to note that liturgy is catechesis in action, "because it is above all a profession of faith and bestowal of grace, and because it is able to produce what it signifies." However, this principle will become operative on condition that the liturgy is woven into the life of the local Church, or, in other words, adapted to its culture and traditions.

Lastly, the liturgy is both a source from which catechesis can draw its material and a point of reference for relating human life and activities to the mystery of Christ and the Church. Sartore suggests that there is no symbol, word, or action in the liturgy that catechists can-

6. D. Sartore, "Catequesis y liturgia," *Nuevo diccionario de liturgia* (Madrid, 1987) 319–332.

not avail themselves of to nourish the faith of their listeners, to invite them to conversion, to build daily the Christian community, and to foster generous service to the Church. In the course of this chapter we shall have occasion to dwell at greater length on this subject. All that we need to say at this point is that the resources owned by the liturgy will have relevance and value for catechesis only if they are able to evoke various life situations, if they are in fact rooted in the culture of the local Church. In short, a liturgy whose expressions are not inculturated has little to offer to a living and effective catechesis.

Over the years there has been a remarkable progress in the relation of liturgy and catechesis. We may say that their interdependence is more firmly established today than in the seventies. Nevertheless, there remain a number of loose ends that call for closer attention.

After the publication of the two apostolic exhortations *Evangelii nuntiandi* and *Catechesi tradendae*, catechists began to focus their interest on the contemporary dimensions of catechesis, sometimes neglecting the patristic and medieval models that are an integral part of its tradition. During the same period, when a large part of the typical editions of the liturgical books was being revised, liturgists showed more concern for preserving the liturgical tradition and reviving the content of medieval liturgical books than in exploring the adequate cultural and pedagogical methods of transmitting the message of the liturgy to the people of our time. But it also happened, and it continues to happen, that in an honest effort to align catechesis with the liturgical year, catechists often transformed it into a kind of liturgical celebration popularly known in the seventies as "paraliturgy." And liturgists who held a one-sided view of the liturgy as "catechesis in action" stressed its catechetical dimensions through running commentaries and exaggerated use of audiovisual aids. In the process, it happened that catechesis and liturgy often got confused with each other and lost something of their identity.[7]

LITURGICAL CATECHESIS IN THE PATRISTIC AGE

Several writings on liturgical catechesis that have come down to us from the patristic age are classic examples of how catechesis should

7. Ibid., 330–331.

relate to the liturgy and to culture. These works belong to pastors and theologians such as Cyril of Jerusalem, John Chrysostom, Theodore of Mopsuestia, Ambrose, and Augustine. Catechesis, which is a form of preaching the word of God, was regarded as the chief task and responsibility of pastors and theologians. Today we often hear the impressive slogan "every Christian is a catechist." There is truth to the statement, but much is required before it can become a reality.

Catechesis and Mystagogy. Scholars like J. Daniélou, A. Trapé, and E. Mazza distinguish between catechesis and mystagogy.[8] Originally catechesis was addressed to those who were about to receive baptism. These were called *illuminandi*, or those who needed to be enlightened first through catechesis before they were enlightened sacramentally by the water of baptism. For in cultural anthropology water enlightens, just as fire washes. In the catechetical discourses of Augustine we observe two types of catechesis, namely the dogmatic, which consisted of the explanation of the Creed, and the moral, which was an instruction on the moral duties of a Christian. Mystagogy was directed to neophytes. It generally comprised the explanation of the sacraments of initiation. The prevailing practice among the Fathers was to expound the meaning of the rites and symbols of the sacraments, that is, the "mysteries," only after they had been celebrated.

Nowadays, the term "mystagogy" is used in reference to the catechetical instruction on the meaning of the sacraments, particularly Christian initiation, and their liturgical rites. Although the *Rite of Christian Initiation of Adults* retains the term "mystagogy" for the postbaptismal instruction of neophytes, people generally interchange "mystagogy" with "catechesis."[9] Mazza, who has written extensively on this subject, informs us that "the broader sense of mystagogy as meaning simply 'explanation of liturgical rites' dates from the beginning of the Byzantine period. It is on the basis of this broader mean-

8. J. Daniélou, *La Catéchèse aux premiers siècles* (Paris, 1968); E. Mazza, *Mystagogy: A Theology of Liturgy in the Patristic Age* (New York, 1989); A. Trapé, "The Catechesis of the Fathers," *GT*, 114–122;
9. *Ordo initiationis Christianae adultorum* (Vatican City, 1972) no. 235; DOL, 753.

ing that mystagogy is applied to every type of liturgical celebration, including priestly ordination and the anointing of the sick."[10]

Two important traits of patristic catechesis deserve closer examination. First, during the patristic age mystagogy, and to some extent also catechesis, possessed a definitely liturgical orientation and purpose. The Fathers always made it a point to draw from the celebration of the sacraments the theological and spiritual doctrine that needed to be explained to the neophytes. Second, the manner or form they employed to expound the doctrine was something we may describe as experiential or culturally evocative, that is, couched in the language and traditions of the listeners. The Fathers we mentioned above were great and profound theological thinkers, but when they spoke to catechumens and neophytes they evoked life situations and alluded to the people's traditions. With inimitable clarity and simplicity they transmitted the most sublime doctrines of Christianity. A. Trapé, who defines catechesis as "the ecclesial ministry destined to transmit the basics of faith," affirms that a great number of the Fathers of the Church were catechists. In fact, they considered themselves to be such, even though they were some of the most learned theologians the Church has ever known. "In reality, they explained the catechism to the flock entrusted to them—to everyone: learned and unlearned, children and adults."[11]

There are two aspects of patristic catechesis whose finer points need to be discussed at greater length, namely, the liturgical basis of catechesis and its cultural evocation. The type of catechesis that has come down to us from the age of the Fathers is a paradigm of how liturgical catechesis should be inculturated.

The Liturgical Basis of Patristic Catechesis. Liturgical catechesis, especially during the fourth and fifth centuries, was of two types. One was the baptismal type addressed to catechumens who were on the final stage of preparation for baptism; the other was the mystagogical type directed to neophytes. Mystagogy consisted of a detailed explanation of the liturgical rites of Christian initiation, which the neophytes received on Easter Vigil. It gave them doctrinal and spiritual

---

10. Mazza, *Mystagogy,* 1.
11. Trapé, "The Catechesis of the Fathers," 114.

insights on what took place when they were being initiated. For a week the bishop gathered them and explained step by step the meaning of the words they heard, the symbols they saw, and the gestures they and the ministers performed. Mystagogy was a review of and a reflection on the previous liturgical celebration. It was meant to assist the neophytes to enter more profoundly into the meaning of the sacraments and to draw from their celebration the spiritual strength they needed to face as Christians the challenges of the world.

Although the "mysteries," that is, the sacraments of initiation, were not explained to the catechumens until after they had been baptized, there was a preparatory type of catechesis consisting of doctrinal and moral instruction. This was part of the long process of faith and conversion, the condition the Church inexorably required for the reception of the sacraments of faith. The celebration of the rites of Christian initiation was the culmination of the process. The mystagogy that followed prolonged for eight days the experience of the mysteries.

The practice of not divulging the content of the awesome rites of Christian initiation must have been motivated by the strict secrecy kept by the Church, then under pagan persecution, regarding the nature of the sacraments. There was much insistence on the *disciplina arcani,* or discipline of secrecy, because of fear that pagans might misunderstand the sacred actions and make a caricature of the Christian sacraments. Nevertheless, when necessary, some Fathers had no qualms about breaking it, even before a pagan audience. Thus, Justin the Martyr revealed the secret concerning the Eucharistic words of Jesus in order to correct pagan misconceptions regarding the Eucharist and to allay doubts about the moral integrity of Christians.[12] The *Rite of Christian Initiation of Adults* still keeps the ancient rule of *disciplina arcani.* It recommends that catechumens, since they are not as yet empowered to participate in Christ's worship, "should be dismissed in a friendly manner before the liturgy of the Eucharist begins, unless there are difficulties in this."[13]

12. Justin the Martyr, *First Apology,* ed. L. Pautigny (Paris, 1904) chs. 61 and 65–67. English trans. by W. Jurgens, *The Faith of the Early Fathers* (Collegeville, 1970) 54–56. Henceforth *FEF.*
13. No. 19,3; DOL, 740.

The *disciplina arcani* explains why in the patristic age the meaning of the sacramental rites was expounded only to the initiated. But apart from this, there seems to be another underlying reason for the practice of mystagogical or postbaptismal catechesis. To grasp more fully the doctrinal and spiritual implications of the sacramental rites, nothing is more helpful than referring to a previous experience of the rites.

BAPTISMAL CATECHESIS. The anonymous author of the *Didachē*, who treats the subject of baptism in chapter 7, provides the readers with some enlightening information regarding the chief elements of the rite of baptism. The author speaks of the Trinitarian formula; the type of water to be used, namely running water; the mode of baptism, which is by immersion; and the immediate preparation through prayer and fasting. For the history of catechesis the first line of chapter 7 has great value: "After the foregoing instructions, baptize in the name of the Father, and of the Son, and of the Holy Spirit, in living water."[14] Though there is still a debate on the complex composition of the book, it would not seem unreasonable to suggest that the "foregoing instructions" actually refer to the preceding six chapters on the "Two Ways." Scholars regard this body of instructions as a Christianized version of the Jewish moral teachings addressed to proselytes. For the author of the *Didachē*, the catechesis preparatory to baptism consists largely of instructions on how to live according to the moral standards set by the Church.

Another author who mentions preparatory catechesis is Justin the Martyr. He reports that "whoever is convinced and believes that what they are taught and told by us is the truth, and professes to be able to live accordingly, is instructed to pray and to beseech God in fasting for the remission of their former sins, while we pray and fast with them. Then they are led by us to a place where there is water."[15] Justin uses here the word *dynamis*, which may be translated as the guts to live according to the true norms of Christian conduct. The candidate is required to manifest not only conviction and faith but also the ability to cope with the situation of persecution then be-

14. *Didachē*, ed. J. Audet (Paris, 1958); *FEF*, 2.
15. Justin the Martyr, *First Apology*, ch. 61; *FEF*, 54.

setting the Church. Thus, as early as the second century the pre-baptismal catechesis included an instruction on the Christian way of life. The period of catechumenate itself was a test of the candidate's fortitude and stamina in the face of pagan persecution as well as formation in the practice of prayer and fasting.

It is in the *Apostolic Tradition* of Hippolytus of Rome that for the first time we come across catechumenate as an organized institution.[16] The author informs us that those who desired to be numbered among the catechumens were brought to the *didaskaloi*, equivalent to our modern-day catechists, in order to ascertain their real motive. They were placed under the care of sponsors or godparents, who would later on give testimony on the worthiness of their lives. Hippolytus enumerates several professions he considered incompatible with being a Christian. He sternly warns candidates to either give up such professions or face rejection by the Church.

Catechumens, according to Hippolytus, "are to listen to the word for three years." This was the standard length of time during which the candidates' gradual conversion could be established. He describes the period of catechumenate as a zealous and faithful listening to the word of God, which was presumably proclaimed in the setting of a liturgical rite. It is true that catechists instructed the catechumens on the practice of Christian morality and that the three years were spent not so much in imparting dogmatic truths and liturgical knowledge as in testing the moral life of candidates. But since the instruction was in the form of "listening to the word," it is most likely that it involved a certain liturgical rite. Hippolytus does not dwell on the details regarding the biblical books, but we know from his contemporary, Origen, that catechists read and explained selected passages from the books of Esther, Judith, Tobit, and Wisdom. These books of Scripture contained suitable moral guidance.[17]

The author of *Apostolic Tradition* mentions standard practices connected with catechetical instruction. A number of these were

16. Hippolytus of Rome, *Apostolic Tradition*, ed. B. Botte (Münster, 1963) ch. 20, pp. 42–44.

17. Origen, *Homilies on the Book of Numbers*, ed. A. Méhat, *Sources chrétiennes* 29 (1951) 27,1. Henceforth *SCh*.

organized following a liturgical orientation and structure. The catechumens were instructed to pray by themselves after each catechetical, or we may correctly say liturgical, session, though they were not offered the kiss of peace, "for their kiss is not yet holy." Kissing was a liturgical gesture, the sign used in the early Church to signify fellowship in baptism and the Eucharist. At the end of the session the catechist, whether clerical or lay, laid hands on each of the catechumens. Again the laying on of hands was a liturgical gesture of blessing.

Sometime before the Easter Vigil—Lent as such did not yet exist—those whom the catechists judged to be ready for baptism were enlisted among the "elect." The patrons were called to testify that the catechumens had lived a worthy life during the time of probation according to the standard established by the Church. Hippolytus asks that "their conduct be examined, whether they respected the widows, visited the sick, and performed every good deed." To probe the sincerity of the elect, the bishop himself exorcised them one by one. Through this liturgical act the bishop was able, in some mysterious way, to perceive their spiritual condition, "because it is not possible for a stranger to pretend at all times." On Holy Thursday the elect washed themselves, and for the next two days they observed the paschal fast. Before baptism the bishop laid hands on them, blew on their faces, and signed their foreheads, ears, and nostrils with the cross. In a sense, all this was part of that process we call catechesis, which was not given as a mere classroom instruction but was done in conjunction with liturgical rites.

The catechesis received by the elect differed in nature and scope from the type given to the other catechumens. The author of *Apostolic Tradition* says that "they should listen to the gospel," but offers no further explanation. We know, however, that by the fourth and fifth centuries the kind of catechesis directed to the elect consisted of a rather thorough and systematic exposition of Sacred Scripture and the Apostles' Creed. Cyril of Jerusalem has left us his eighteen catechetical instructions, which he delivered to the elect before the Easter triduum of 349. Among other things, they deal with baptism, penance, the nature and origin of faith, the books of Sacred Scripture, and the articles of the Creed concerning the Father, the Son, the Holy Spirit, the Church, the resurrection of the dead, and eternal life.[18] From the instruction given by Hippolytus that the elect "should listen to the gospel" we may infer again that catechesis was delivered in the setting of a liturgical rite.

From the foregoing discussion we draw the conclusion that in the patristic period there were two forms of catechesis preparatory to the celebration of baptism. The first was given to catechumens for a period of about three years. It was basically an instruction on the kind of life the Church required of its members. The patristic literature we have examined seems to lay the stress, at this stage, on the moral qualification of catechumens. The sponsors followed up the instruction given by the catechists and, at the conclusion of the catechumenate, testified before the Church regarding the worthiness of the candidates. The catechists played the role of spiritual directors who guided the catechumens on the way of Christian conduct. They taught them how to pray. They read and explained the Scriptures to them, and blessed them at the end of each session. On account of this, we should not hesitate to regard the catechetical sessions during the patristic age as liturgical rites. In fact, they followed the format of the Liturgy of the Word, consisting of reading from Scripture, instruction, prayer, and blessing.

The other form of catechesis was reserved to the elect, who had been chosen to receive the sacraments of initiation. This stage of the catechumenate initiated them into a more systematic understanding of the revealed truths. The Church, during the patristic age, furnished it with liturgical rites, especially as the day of baptism approached. The systematic instruction on Christian doctrine was never a cold and abstract exposition of dogmatic truths. It came alive in the celebration of liturgical rites. It would indeed be difficult to imagine an explanation of Christian doctrine, especially when it is addressed to those who are preparing to receive the sacraments of initiation, that ignores the connection between liturgy and dogma.

The culmination of the period of catechetical instruction and spiritual formation came at the Easter celebration of baptism, confirmation, and Holy Eucharist. Although the candidates were as yet ignorant of the full meaning and details of the liturgical rites, they were spiritually and morally ready for them. For eight days following

18. Cyril of Jerusalem, *Catechetical Lectures*; portions in *FEF*, 347–359.

146

the celebration they gathered around the bishop to review the experience of the Easter night and draw new doctrinal and spiritual insights from it.

MYSTAGOGICAL CATECHESIS. Liturgical catechesis was given to neophytes in the form of mystagogy. Mazza has made an excellent study of the mystagogical treatises of Ambrose, Theodore of Mopsuestia, John Chrysostom, and Cyril of Jerusalem. His rigorous analysis of the vocabulary used by each of these writers throws light on the meaning they attached to the liturgical rites of Christian initiation and on the method they adopted when they explained the rites to neophytes. Though biblical typology was still much at work in the mystagogy of the Fathers of the fourth and fifth centuries, Mazza believes that it began to show signs of decline in the works he has studied. He claims that at certain moments the mystagogical theology of these Fathers already makes room for a "theology of the mysteries," which views the liturgical rite as the "presence" of the saving event.[19]

Paradoxically, biblical typology and mystery theology are the two hinges around which the liturgy, especially of the sacraments, revolves. The text for the blessing of the baptismal water, for example, lines up an array of biblical types. It recalls the water on which the Spirit breathed at the dawn of creation, the water of the great flood, the water of the Red Sea, the water of the Jordan where Christ was baptized by John, and the water that flowed from the side of Christ. The reason why the Church commemorates these events, or in technical terms, makes an anamnesis of them, is in order to announce that the figures have now at last become a reality in the sacrament of baptism. The idea is highlighted in the following portions of the formulary for the blessing of baptismal water: "The waters of the great flood you made a sign of the waters of baptism, that make an end of sin and a new beginning of goodness"; "Through the waters of the Red Sea you led Israel out of slavery, to be an image of God's holy people, set free from sin by baptism."[20]

19. Mazza, *Mystagogy,* ix–xii.
20. *Ordo initiationis Christianae adultorum,* no. 215; English text in *The Rites,* (New York, 1976) 1:96–98.

The orations after the Old Testament readings at the Easter Vigil are texts that the Church drew up having in mind the biblical types as God's promises and the sacraments of initiation as the presence and fulfillment of those promises. Biblical typology and mystery theology go hand in hand in these orations. Three representative texts give clear utterance to what is on the mind of the Church. We read in the first oration: "You created all things in wonderful beauty and order. Help us now to perceive how still more wonderful is the new creation by which in the fullness of time you redeemed your people through the sacrifice of our passover, Jesus Christ." We meet the same idea in the second and third orations. The second oration reads: "You promised Abraham that he would become the father of all nations, and through the death and resurrection of Christ you fulfill that promise: everywhere throughout the world you increase your chosen people." The third oration is explicitly sacramental in its application of the biblical type to its antitype: "Even today we see the wonders of the miracles you worked long ago. You once saved a single nation from slavery, and now you offer that salvation to all through baptism."[21] We may say that this interplay between biblical types and the Christian mystery, between promise and fulfillment, is the heart of liturgical anamnesis.

But what part in the process of inculturating sacramental catechesis does biblical typology play? Inculturation is a type of dynamic translation. It involves the process of admitting into the liturgy such cultural elements and values as are able to illustrate the meaning of the sacramental rite. These elements root the celebration in the cultural expressions of the people; they make it, in effect, part of their life experience. However, they have no biblical underpinnings; they are an alien segment in the liturgical rite, whose ultimate foundation is the word of God. How then can they be made to interact with the Christian mystery, which the liturgy celebrates? The answer the Fathers would have given is through biblical typology. This means in concrete terms that the cultural elements receive a new interpretation, a new meaning, and a new dimension from the saving event narrated in Sacred Scripture. It means that native cultural rites, symbols, and

21. *The Sacramentary* (New York, 1974) 188–189.

values acquire a new character, status, and purpose: now they convey the message of the sacraments in the light of salvation history.

The value of biblical typology for both liturgy and catechesis cannot be overestimated. The mystagogical writings of the Fathers expertly combine biblical typology and mystery theology and reveal a penetrating insight on the meaning of the liturgical rites. At the same time, they furnish us with models of catechetical instruction that are undoubtedly some of the finest examples of how, on the basis of the biblical types, our own liturgical catechesis can successfully be inculturated in the particular context of a local Church.

The mystagogical writings of Ambrose of Milan and Cyril of Jerusalem are two of the classic examples of this type of catechesis. In Ambrose's *On Mysteries* and *On Sacraments* and in Cyril's *Mystagogical Catechesis* we observe how these two Fathers constantly make references to the celebration of the rites of initiation.[22] They review step by step what took place during the celebration and explain the prayers, gestures, and symbols that made up the liturgical rite. In a manner that became typical of patristic catechesis, they delve into the biblical types in order to bring out the hidden plan of God. This plan, they assure the neophytes, was finally revealed and fulfilled by Christ and now has become operative in the sacraments of the Church. Thus, biblical typology, which is highly prized by liturgical and patristic tradition, links the celebration of the sacraments to the history of salvation and, as it were, plunges the neophytes into the stream of God's saving plan.

The mystagogical treatises of Ambrose are representative of this method of instructing neophytes. Throughout these two works he employs the experiential approach. To explain, for example, the seriousness of baptismal renunciation, Ambrose starts by recalling what took place on Easter night: "When you were asked, 'Do you renounce the devil and his works?' what did you reply? 'I do renounce.' 'Do you renounce the world and its pleasures?' what did you answer? 'I do renounce.'" He then instills in the neophytes the serious character of the baptismal promises, which they made in the form of a pledge:

22. Ambrose of Milan, *On Sacraments* and *On Mysteries*, ed. B. Botte; *SCh* 25bis (1961); Cyril of Jerusalem, *Mystagogical Catechesis*, ed. A. Piédagnel; *SCh* 125 (1966); see Mazza, *Mystagogy*, 14–44, 150–164.

"Always remember what you promised and never lose sight of the consequences of the pledge you made."[23]

Regarding the baptismal water, Ambrose first of all refreshes the memory of the neophytes: "You entered, you saw the water, you saw the bishop, you saw the deacon. Perhaps someone has said, 'Is this all there is to it?'" With this question he begins to unravel the mystery, that is, the sacrament, of water. "Yes," he replies, "this is all, for here we find innocence, here we find devotion, grace, and sanctification."[24] Similarly, before he explains the symbolism of immersion, he first re-creates what happened at the moment of baptism: "You were asked, 'Do you believe in God the Father Almighty?' You answered, 'I believe,' and you dipped, that is, you were buried."[25]

The experiential approach made it possible for Ambrose to make a leap from the reality of liturgical rite to the realm of doctrine and spirituality. Such a leap, however, was made possible for him by the method of biblical typology. Thus, to explain the meaning of baptismal water he recalls those instances recorded in Sacred Scripture when water foreshadowed the saving water of baptism: the water at the time of creation over which the Spirit hovered, the flood in the time of Noah, the water of the Red Sea, the bitter water made sweet by Moses, the water of the Jordan that cleansed Naaman from leprosy, and the pool of Bethsaida where the paralytic was cured.[26] For Ambrose these biblical types are meant to engrave in the mind of the neophytes a sense of continuity between God's promise and its fulfillment in the Church. They are meant to impart the truth that baptism is the realization of the plan of salvation, which God gradually unfolded in the course of history.

This manner of using Sacred Scripture for purposes of catechetical instruction should not lead us to believe that biblical types are some handy pedagogical material that we can conveniently employ to create a biblical setting for catechesis. Biblical types are the means of in-

23. Ambrose of Milan, *On Sacraments,* 1,5; SCh, 62.
24. Ibid., 1,10, pp. 64–66.
25. Ibid., 2,20, pp. 84–86.
26. Ambrose of Milan, *On Mysteries,* 3,9, p. 160 (water of creation); 3,10–11, pp. 160–162 (the deluge); 3,12–13, p. 162 (the Exodus); 3,14, p. 162 (bitter water); 3,16, p. 164 (Naaman); 3,21, p. 166 (pool of Bethsaida).

serting both the human dimensions and natural elements of the sacraments in the scheme of salvation history. That is why the type of catechesis that ignores biblical types and substitutes them exclusively with images taken from daily life runs the risk of lifting out the celebration of the sacraments from the stream of salvation history. Inculturated catechesis does not mean neglecting biblical types in favor of anecdotes from daily life about water or oil, however relevant to the occasion these anecdotes might be. It means associating biblical types with contemporary events, rites, and symbols. It means reading the biblical types in the light of the history, culture, and traditions of the local Church.

Ambrose does not indulge in biblical types merely to commemorate past events in salvation history. He shifts his attention from type to antitype, from figure to reality, from mystagogical theology to mystery theology. The types prefigure the work God accomplished through Christ. The wonders God performed for his chosen people Israel are mere shadows of the reality we call the sacraments of the Church. Referring to the Spirit who hovered over the water of creation, Ambrose muses: "Did he who moved over the water [of creation] not work also on the water [of baptism]?"[27] The Holy Spirit, who breathed life into the creatures of the water at the dawn of time, now breathes divine life into those who are immersed in the water of baptism. The Holy Spirit of creation is now present in the sacramental rites of the Church.

The explanation Ambrose makes regarding the action of the Holy Spirit on the baptismal font is an impressive example of how mystagogy turns into mystery, and how the promise becomes a present reality. In lapidary words he writes: "If then the Holy Spirit, coming upon the Virgin, brought about conception and birth, surely there must be no doubt that the same Spirit, coming upon the font, or upon those who are baptized, brings about rebirth."[28] Ambrose regards the role played by the Holy Spirit in the mystery of the incarnation as a foreshadowing of his role in the sacrament of rebirth. He sees the Blessed Mother as figure of the Church, and her womb as the type of the baptismal font of the Church. He draws a striking

27. Ibid., 3,9, p. 160.
28. Ibid., 9,59, p. 192.

parallel between the spiritual rebirth of neophytes and the mystery of Christ's incarnation.

From Ambrose we learn that the aim of mystagogy is not only to teach sacramental theology but also to communicate spiritual insights to neophytes. Mystagogy was part of the early Church's program of spiritual formation. Just as sacramental theology was based on the celebration of the liturgical rites, so also spirituality was rooted in the sacramental experience of neophytes. According to Ambrose, spirituality is nothing else but the faithful living out of the consequences of the sacraments. In sublime and moving words he preached to his neophytes, exhorting them to remain faithful to the end: "When you dip in the water, you take on the likeness of Christ's death and burial, you accept the sacrament of that cross on which he hung and to which his body was nailed. You then are crucified with Christ, you cling to him, you cling to the nails of the Lord Jesus Christ. Let not the devil take you down from it. Let the nails of Christ hold you whom the weakness of human nature disengages."[29]

From the foregoing discussion we conclude that during the patristic age baptismal catechesis and mystagogy posssessed a liturgical orientation. While certain liturgical rites accompanied baptismal catechesis, the three sacraments of initiation were themselves the subject matter of mystagogy. Since our area of interest is models of liturgical inculturation, it would be useful to recall at this point those elements of patristic mystagogy that constitute the catechetical and liturgical *terminus a quo* of inculturation.

In the writings of Ambrose we observe his frequent utilization of biblical types. It would seem that in the process of inculturation these should be retained, though read and expounded in the light of contemporary culture, because they are able to relate the sacraments to salvation history. We likewise observe how Ambrose constantly shifts from biblical types to sacramental antitypes, from promise to fulfillment, in short, from mystagogical theology to mystery theology. Lastly, we observe that he bases his reflections on Christian spirituality on the celebration and personal experience of the sacraments. These are the chief traits of liturgical catechesis during the patristic

29. Ambrose of Milan, *On Sacraments*, 2,24, p. 88.

period. The question ahead of us is how to translate them into the culture and traditions of local Churches.

Cultural Evocation in Patristic Catechesis. An aspect of patristic catechesis with significant and practical implications for inculturation is the quality that enables it to evoke cultural settings and link them to the liturgical rites and biblical types. The patristic form of catechesis relied heavily on culture for its material. Apropos, Pope John Paul II affirms that catechesis, as well as evangelization in general, "is called to bring the power of the Gospel into the very heart of culture and cultures." This will be realized on condition that catechists seek to know these cultures and their essential components, that they learn the most significant expressions of culture, and that they respect their particular values and riches.[30] The Pope encourages certain elements, religious or otherwise, that form part of a people's cultural heritage to be used with discernment in order to promote a better understanding of the faith. He warns, however, against "renunciation or obscuring of its message, by adaptations, even in language, that would endanger the 'precious deposit' of faith."[31]

A point that has direct relevance to our subject is raised by Pope John Paul II in *Catechesi tradendae.* There is a need to maintain the link of catechesis to the biblical world as well as to the other cultures in the past, or, in short, to Church tradition. In the work of inculturating liturgical catechesis in the setting of our present-day society, tradition should not be overlooked. The long passage in which the Pope articulates his thinking on the subject is worth reproducing here. "The Gospel message cannot be purely and simply isolated from the culture in which it was first inserted (the biblical world or, more concretely, the cultural milieu in which Jesus of Nazareth lived), nor, without serious loss, from the cultures in which it has already been expressed down the centuries; it does not spring spontaneously from any cultural soil; it has always been transmitted by means of an apostolic dialogue which inevitably becomes part of a certain dialogue of cultures."[32]

30. John Paul II, *Catechesi tradendae,* no. 53, p. 667.
31. Ibid., 668.
32. Ibid., 667.

The catechetical writings of the Fathers are a record of that "apostolic dialogue" between the content of faith and the expressions of culture. The cultural setting was the Greco-Roman world in the fourth and fifth centuries. It is obvious that a good number of the examples coming from this period will not make sense to people who belong to another culture and age, perhaps even the modern Europeans. Because of the particular cultural patterns underlying the patristic models, they have distanced themselves from the normal life experience of the people of today. This does not mean that they have altogether lost relevance. However, to appreciate what they can contribute to modern catechesis we need to make a certain distinction, namely between the origin of the liturgical rites and the catechetical interpretation they received from the Fathers. A number of liturgical rites originated in the culture of the local Church. If by "local Church" we mean also the Church of Jerusalem, then of course all liturgical rites sprang from a local cultural ambient. The question is how the Fathers interpreted them, that is, vested them with contemporary cultural expression so that they could be inserted into the living tradition of the local Church. In short, how did the Fathers evoke culture when they explained the meaning of liturgical rites?

Cultural evocation in catechesis occurs rather frequently in the mystagogical treatises of the early Fathers. One example is the method Ambrose adopted in order to explain the rite of anointing the catechumens immediately before they were baptized. He made recourse to a current practice of rubbing athletes with oil, a kind of body massage, in preparation for the competition. It was a commonplace among Greeks and Romans, as it is also among us today, to apply oil for body conditioning. Ambrose was quick to see in the baptismal anointing of catechumens a rite comparable to the athletic practice in his day. Catechumens, after all, had to be prepared to face the trials ahead of them. This explains why the reminder Ambrose gave to the neophytes is couched in words evoking the world of athletes: "You were anointed as an athlete of Christ, as one who is about to fight the battle of this world, as one who has given oneself to battle. One who enters the contest knows what to expect: where there is struggle, there is crown."[33]

33. Ambrose of Milan, *On Sacraments*, 1,4, p. 62.

It would not be pure fantasy to think that the rite of baptismal anointing could have been inspired by the practice of athletes. According to B. Botte, there is no indication of such a rite in the New Testament and in the writings of the Fathers before Tertullian.[34] It is quite possible that Ambrose tried to retrieve the original idea behind the rite. However, when he explained its meaning, he joined it up with 1 Corinthians 9:24–27, which describes Christian life as a race in the arena.

Another example where we see cultural evocation at work is the rite of baptismal renunciation. For the people of the ancient Mediterranean world the directions east and west were particularly rich in symbolism. On this subject F. Dölger has written profusely.[35] The early Christians turned toward the east when they prayed in the belief that Christ who went up to heaven to the east would return also from the direction of the east. The *Apostolic Tradition* directs the catechumens to face the west at the moment of renunciation (one manuscript adds spitting toward the west) and to face the east at the profession of faith.[36] The west or the region where the sun sets signifies the domain of Satan, while the east is where Christ reigns. Ambrose has captured the symbolism in these graphic words: "Having entered [the baptistery] to encounter your adversary whom you decided to renounce to his face, you turned toward the east. For those who renounce the devil, turn toward Christ and recognize him by a direct glance."[37]

Two other baptismal rites, both extinct, have strong cultural underpinnings. These are the washing of the feet of neophytes and the giving of the cup of milk mixed with honey at their first Communion. P. Beatrice has published an interesting study on the washing of feet.[38]

34. B. Botte, "Le symbolisme de l'huile et de l'onction," *Questions Liturgiques* 4 (1981) 196. Tertullian himself declares in *The Crown*, 3,1: Hanc [unctionem] si nulla scriptura determinavit, certe consuetudo corroboravit, quae sine dubio de traditione manavit."

35. F. Dölger, *Sol Salutis: Gebet und Gesang im christlichen Altertum* (Münster, 1972); see J. Jungmann, *The Early Liturgy to the Time of Gregory the Great* (London, 1966) 133–139.

36. Hippolytus of Rome, *Apostolic Tradition*, ch. 21, p. 46.

37. Ambrose of Milan, *On Mysteries*, 2,7, p. 158.

38. P. Beatrice, *La lavanda dei piedi* (Rome, 1983).

In the ancient Roman and Milanese liturgies there existed a rather curious practice of washing the feet of neophytes after they had been baptized. How it became part of the baptismal rite is a question too complex to discuss here. In the time of Ambrose, the Church of Milan still kept the practice, though Rome had abandoned it because it had become unwieldy on account of the large number of catechumens who were being baptized. What could have been the cultural background of this practice?

For a people who did a lot of walking washing the feet was a practical gesture of welcome and hospitality. It was a menial task assigned to servants. This seems to be the spirit behind chapter 53 of *The Rule of Saint Benedict,* which enjoins the abbot and the community to wash the feet of the newly arrived guests. This cultural background was surely not lost to Ambrose, who was quite sensitive to the cultural and social traditions of his people. However, he explains this peculiar rite as an act of humble service, in accord with John 13:5–10, and as a sacramental act whose effect complements baptism. Alluding to Genesis 3:15, which speaks of the serpent striking at the heel, Ambrose gives the rite yet another interpretation: "Your feet were washed in order to wash away the venom of the serpent."[39]

The other initiation rite that did not withstand the test of time and cultural change is the rather charming practice of offering a cup of milk mixed with honey to neophytes at their first Communion. Ancient Rome knew the tradition of making newly born infants drink a mixture of milk and honey for strength against sickness or as an apotropaic ritual to ward off evil.[40] Tertullian reports that in the Church of North Africa the neophytes drank, soon after baptism, a mixture of milk and honey to signify that they have been received by the Church. The *Apostolic Tradition* inserts the practice between Communion with the bread and Communion from the cup. To avoid any gross misunderstanding that might arise regarding the nature of the mixed drink at the time of Communion, Hippolytus directs "the bishop to explain its meaning carefully to those who receive it." In the light of Exodus 3:8, he interprets the mixed drink as "the fulfillment of the promise given by God to our fathers, that he would give

39. Ambrose of Milan, *On Sacraments,* 3,4–7, p. 96.
40. See Pauly-Wissowa, ed., *Real-Encyclopedie* 30 (1931) 1570–1571.

them a land flowing with milk and honey." The biblical type fits nicely with the cup of milk and honey. Through the rite of baptism the neophytes cross the river Jordan; they enter the land of spiritual abundance promised by God, that is, the Church. The mixed drink is the symbol signifying the fruition of the promise.[41]

The foregoing examples of cultural evocation in patristic mystagogy direct our attention to a significant fact. The remarkable ease with which the Fathers linked culture to the sacraments has only one explanation: the liturgy of the sacraments was in fact inculturated, that is, it possessed elements borrowed from the life experience of the people. The practice of rubbing oil, the east and west direction, the washing of feet, the cup of milk and honey, the use of the white garment, and the giving of lighted candles—these were familiar things in the culture of the early Church. The Fathers did not have to search outside the liturgy for a ritual or an imagery that could aptly illustrate the meaning of the sacramental rites. The liturgy already contained the material for a catechesis that imaginatively re-created aspects of a people's collective experience. While the biblical types inserted the sacramental rites into the realm of salvation history, the cultural elements rooted them in the life of the local Church.

Thus, both catechesis and liturgy spoke the same language, referred to the same cultural setting, and transmitted, using the same pedagogy, the content of the sacraments. In other words, the sacramental liturgy and its corresponding catechesis were not merely juxtaposed. The examples given above are not the result of acculturation. For what takes place when there is acculturation is that catechists adopt the experiential approach to explain the sacraments but are not able to draw material from the liturgical rites and hence fail to show the relationship between liturgy and life experience. As we have seen, in their catechetical and mystagogical treatises the Fathers furnish us with paradigms of an inculturated catechesis. Owing to the inculturated rites and symbols of the sacraments of initiation during the patristic age, the concomitant explanations could easily allude to the people's cultural traditions. The conclusion is that so long

41. Tertullian, *The Crown*, 3,2; *FEF*, 151. Hippolytus of Rome, *Apostolic Tradition*, ch. 21, p. 56.

as our liturgy is not inculturated, our liturgical catechesis can attain only the level of acculturation.

CATECHESIS AND THE TYPICAL EDITIONS

Liturgical catechesis draws its instructional material from the liturgical and sacramental activity of the Church. The material is provided by the texts, rites, and symbols used in liturgical celebrations. These are strictly the inalienable foundation of liturgical catechesis. Abstract theological considerations concerning the liturgy and the sacraments have surely a distinct value of their own for the formation of Christians, but liturgical catechesis means more than mere intellectual enrichment. It should lead the faithful to the celebration of the sacraments and to an experience of their effect in life. Genuine liturgical catechesis is never mere abstract or classroom information on the Church's worship; it is always a lively experiential unfolding of the faith the Church celebrates.[42]

A Contemporary Mystagogical Approach. With respect to liturgical orientation, the *De Nieuwe Katechismus,* commonly known as the Dutch *Catechism,* deserves high commendation.[43] Its treatise on the sacraments of baptism and the Eucharist is a faithful presentation of the liturgical celebrations from which it draws profound and often moving reflections on the meaning these sacraments should have for modern-day believers.[44] Going over its pages, one receives the distinct impression of reading a modern version of patristic mystagogy.

The following lines from the *Catechism* could easily be attributed to Ambrose of Milan. Speaking of baptism as the new birth, the *Catechism* explains: "The water signifies birth, the words specify what birth it is, namely, that the Holy Spirit enters into us, gives us life and makes us children of the Father. Immediately after baptism there is an anointing with chrism, which signifies the good odor of the Spirit."[45] Concerning the aspect of baptism as the symbol of our solidarity with Christ's own way of service, humility, and obedience

42. See Sartore, "Catequesis y Liturgia," 319–332.
43. The English translation carries the title *A New Catechism* (New York, 1967).
44. Ibid., 242–248; 332–347.
45. Ibid., 245.

even unto death, the *Catechism* has these inspiring and animating words: "Is this a sombre thought on the happy day of baptism—that one is thereby dedicated to death? But is there anything more consoling? We are reminded that our mortal life is to be, along with Jesus, not absurd but fruitful. God has turned the woes of mankind into the birthpangs of new life. When we enter the water, it is a symbol of death; when we leave it, it is the symbol of resurrection and rebirth. That is why baptism is conferred on the happy night of Easter."[46]

Whenever the Dutch *Catechism* addresses the subject of liturgy, it echoes faithfully the plan and content of the typical editions of the liturgical books. However, it does not neglect the spiritual and devotional dimensions of the celebration. Commenting on the narration of the institution as the climax of the Mass, it notes the silence observed by the assembly during this solemn occasion. Before the reform many of the faithful made the sign of the cross and beat their breasts, but now we only look upward to adore the consecrated species. And as we do so, "some say silently to themselves the paschal words of the Apostle Thomas, 'My Lord and my God!' One could also repeat some of the words on Calvary, such as, 'This is indeed the Son of God.' Or one need say nothing at all. The basic effort must always be to remember Jesus Christ. The consecration is a holy and privileged moment in the canon. But the whole canon shares in this holiness."[47]

The Typical Editions and the Task of Catechists. The texts, rites, and symbols of the liturgy are the starting point for the inculturation not only of liturgical rites but also of liturgical catechesis. The typical editions of the various liturgical books should be part of the process of adapting liturgical catechesis to the culture of local Churches. The typical editions, which determine what may be changed or modified in the texts or rites of the liturgy, can inspire catechists to consider how certain elements of the celebration could be linked with cultural expressions. Thus, the introduction to the typical editions names the occasions when the conferences of bishops or the minister may adapt

46. Ibid., 247.
47. Ibid., 335.

the texts or the rites of the liturgy.[48] We should point out here that the options offered to the bishops are options the catechists should learn to convert to the advantage of their work of catechetical instruction. Without introducing changes in the rite—this is the domain of the conferences of bishops—they should be alert to the possibility of explaining the meaning of a liturgical rite in the light of the cultural options the typical editions offer to bishops.

Apropos of methodology, it would be useful to consider briefly what constitutes the content and form of liturgical catechesis. We may say that the content of liturgical catechesis is basically the theological meaning of the sacraments or liturgical actions embodied in the corresponding liturgical rites. We may say further that the paschal mystery, which is made present in every liturgical celebration, is in fact the principal meaning of the rite. However, we should note that at Holy Mass the focus is on Christ's sacrifice on the cross, at baptism on his burial and resurrection, and at confirmation on his act of sending the Holy Spirit to the Church on the day of Pentecost. In short, every sacrament contains, signifies, and celebrates the paschal mystery according to the particular nature and purpose of the sacrament. Thus, in the Eucharist the meal with bread and wine is the liturgical rite expressing the presence of the paschal mystery, in baptism the washing with water and the Trinitarian formula, and in confirmation the laying on of hands and anointing with chrism. The typical editions indicate quite clearly the nature and purpose of each liturgical celebration. At the outset we should warn catechists that the theological meaning of the rite is not the object of catechetical inculturation if this would involve changing the meaning of the sacrament.

The form of catechesis, however, consists in what Pope John Paul II calls the "suitable ways and means" and the "suitable pedagogical methods" of communicating the content or message of catechesis.[49] The Pope suggests that the traditional language used in catechesis may have to give way to another language that might prove "preferable for transmitting the content to a particular individual or group."

48. See A. Chupungco, *Liturgies of the Future: The Process and Methods of Inculturation* (New York, 1989) 122–154.
49. John Paul II, *Catechesi tradendae*, nos. 31 and 46, pp. 651, 662.

He underlines "the great possibilities offered by the means of social communication and the means of group communication: television, radio, the press, records, tape recordings—the whole series of audio-visual means."

What, then, is the object of inculturation? Catechists do not, of course, enjoy the right to inculturate the rites of the sacraments and other liturgical actions. This is a task assigned by the Holy See exclusively to the conferences of bishops. The task of catechists is to inculturate the language, methods, and pedagogical means of catechesis in view of explaining, in the setting of culture and traditions of their people, the theological content and liturgical forms of the rites. Pope John Paul II defines genuine catechists as teachers who know "that catechesis 'takes flesh' in the various cultures and milieux."[50] He reminds them that the form of communication "must be linked with the real life of the generation to which it is addressed," and that "it must try to speak a language comprehensible to the generation in question."[51]

Thus, in their own way catechists perform the task of theologians when they transmit sound theological doctrine on the meaning and purpose of the sacraments. They share the expertise of liturgists by being sufficiently informed about the historical background of the rites, the meaning of the myriad liturgical gestures and symbols, and the theological and spiritual content of the different liturgical books. They do the work of pastors who lead their listeners to a more profound appreciation of the liturgical celebrations, so that "they may hold fast in their lives to what they have grasped by their faith." In this rather formidable list of qualities we should include keen sensitivity to culture and traditions together with the genius for making dynamic cultural translations of the liturgical rites. There is no doubt that liturgical catechesis will be relevant to our times to the extent that catechists are able to inculturate or at least acculturate their instructional material and methods. The inculturation of liturgical catechesis is surely not an option but an imperative.

With this observation in mind, the *National Catechetical Directory for the Philippines* has issued an urgent call to spare no effort so that

50. Ibid., no. 53, p. 668.
51. Ibid., no. 49, p. 665.

the form and methods of catechetical instruction might be effectively inculturated. "On the one hand," the *Directory* enjoins, "the Christian message must be expressed through images, symbols, rites that are indigenous to Philippine culture, and on the other, authentic Filipino cultural values, attitudes, and practices must be analyzed for their basic Christian dimensions."[52] The *Directory*, which frankly admits that the inculturation of catechesis cannot be a process accomplished by decree from on high, invites the local Church to find the forms and expressions in worship and life that are "both distinctly Filipino and authentically Christian." It points out that the liturgical celebrations and popular devotions offer the best available opportunities for inculturation. It warns, however, that "inculturation is more than 'clothing' the message in indigenous symbols, rites, and forms. More fundamentally it is the deeper, interior insight and understanding of Christ Jesus which becomes part of the Filipino 'soul.'"[53]

The *Directory*, which takes inspiration from Pope Paul VI's *Evangelii nuntiandi*, Pope John Paul II's *Catechesi tradendae*, and the *Document of Puebla*, was written in the cultural setting of the local Church, but several of the issues it addresses are cross-cultural. In many ways, other local Churches and communities in the West sharing the same Latin form of Catholicism can readily identify with the concerns articulated in the *Directory*.

The Options Offered by the Typical Editions. The problem catechists have to grapple with is how to begin in concrete terms the course of the inculturation or acculturation of liturgical catechesis. In other words, what methods are available. To answer this question it is necessary to return to the subject of the typical editions, the official source of liturgical catechesis and *terminus a quo* of inculturation. The various options they offer to the conferences of bishops can help catechists immensely in their arduous task of infusing cultural perceptivity into liturgical celebrations. A couple of examples using the typical editions will illustrate the point.

In the general introduction to *Christian Initiation* we come across the option given to conferences of bishops "to retain distinctive ele-

52. *Maturing in Christian Faith* (Pasay City, 1985) no. 426, p. 226.
53. Ibid., no. 431, p. 228.

ments of any existing local rituals, as long as they conform to the Constitution on the Liturgy and correspond to contemporary needs."[54] Even in the event that this had not been implemented when the new particular ritual was drawn up, catechists can nonetheless incorporate into their instructional material the "distinctive elements" that can add local color to the revised rite of baptism. These elements may have something to do with the special role given by local tradition to godparents, the giving of the "salt of wisdom," the signing of the various parts of the child's body: forehead, ears, eyes, nose, mouth, breast, and shoulders, the laying of the stole on the child, and the particular shape and color of the baptismal garment.

The general introduction to *Christian Initiation* offers another option already mentioned in *SC* 65: "The conferences of bishops in mission countries have the responsibility to judge whether certain initiation ceremonies in use among some peoples can be adapted for the rite of Christian baptism."[55] The conferences of bishops will decide whether these native initiation ceremonies are to be incorporated into the rite of baptism. But even before any decision on the matter is reached catechists should consider how such ceremonies can root the sacrament of baptism in the people's initiatory traditions and thus enrich their understanding of it. What we are dealing with here is, in a sense, something akin to the place the postbaptismal anointing with chrism, vesting in the white garment, and the giving of lighted candles hold in the liturgy of baptism. These illustrate the meaning and consequences of the sacrament. In a similar fashion native initiation rites can, as cultural references for liturgical catechesis, illustrate the meaning of the Christian mystery.

Among the many options offered by the typical edition, those pertaining to the rite of marriage merit particular attention.[56] In the introduction to the typical edition of the marriage rite we come across a number of possible changes the conferences of bishops may intro-

54. *Ordo initiationis Christianae adultorum* (Vatican City, 1974) no. 30,2; *DOL,* 724.
55. *Ordo initiationis Christianae adultorum,* no. 31, DOL, 724. See Chupungco, *Liturgies of the Future,* 128–130.
56. *Ordo celebrandi matrimonium* (Vatican City, 1991) 4, nos. 39–44. English text, where applicable, in *DOL,* 923–924. See Chupungco, *Liturgies of the Future,* 139–149.

duce into the particular ritual. Examples are the crowning or veiling of the bride, omission or substitution with other rites of the joining of hands and the exchange of rings, and the assimilation of native marriage customs, provided they are not indissolubly bound up with superstition and error and can be made to harmonize with the true and authentic spirit of the liturgy.[57] Where applicable, these and other options, whether they are received in the particular ritual or not, are materials catechists can amply utilize as local illustrations of the nature and purpose of the sacrament of marriage. Due to the ritual and textual sobriety of the rite of marriage, even in its 1991 typical edition, it can require considerable dexterity and imagination to draw from it adequate material for liturgical catechesis. It is necessary for catechists to have recourse to local customs, traditions, and values that are not in fact part of the sacramental rite but are nonetheless able to enrich the people's understanding of marriage.

A final example is the option to use another type of oil in place of olive oil for the sacrament of the sick, provided it is derived from plants.[58] Pope Paul VI, who introduced this most welcome and in a sense revolutionary change in the discipline of the sacrament, justified it on practical and pastoral grounds. In the apostolic constitution promulgating the revised rite he explains that "since olive oil, which has been prescribed until now for the valid celebration of the sacrament, is unobtainable or difficult to obtain in some parts of the world, we have decreed, at the request of a number of bishops, that from now on, according to circumstances, another kind of oil can also be used, provided it is derived from plants and is thus similar to olive oil."[59]

The option has practical implications for liturgical catechesis. There are regions in the world where olive oil is practically unheard of. It can take some considerable effort to explain what it is and why it is used for the sick instead of the local coconut oil or, in the context of popular religiosity, the oil from the lamps burning before the images of saints. In some places people use for the sick a kind of oil derived

57. *Ordo celebrandi matrimonium*, 4, nos. 41–42; *DOL*, nos. 15–16, p. 924.
58. *Ordo unctionis infirmorum* (Vatican City, 1975) no. 20; *DOL*, 1057. See Chupungco, *Liturgies of the Future*, 151–154.
59. Paul VI, *Sacram unctionem infirmorum; DOL*, 1052.

from plants known particularly for their medicinal quality. Around this tradition, stories recalling divine intervention or the community's concern toward the sick have grown in the course of time. These stories are handed down from one generation to the next, and catechists can surely avail themselves of such stories to contextualize the message of Christ's and the Church's concern for the sick.

The foregoing examples establish the importance of the typical editions in the inculturation or acculturation of liturgical catechesis. In a sense, the typical editions are the practical point of departure for the inculturation of both the particular ritual and liturgical catechesis. It would be useful to stress once again, even to the point of being repetitious, that inculturation does not consist in creating a completely new rite but in translating the content of the Roman Rite into the cultural patterns of the local Church.

Similarly, the inculturation of liturgical catechesis does not reside in the creative production of paraliturgies in disregard for the liturgical rites presented by the typical editions. Catechists who use paraliturgies could run the risk of disengaging liturgical catechesis from the liturgy. Celebrating paraliturgies in order to explain the meaning of the sacraments can only lead to an unhealthy tension and to estrangement. As a result, the sacraments can become even more alienated from the religious experience of the community and thus unable to affect and evangelize its cultural pattern. But apart from this consideration, the typical editions, as the above examples have shown, can serve as springboards for the inculturation of catechesis, as they in fact do for the inculturation of the liturgical rites.

The typical editions can guide the course of liturgical catechesis, but they are not the sole factor for the success of inculturation or acculturation. A measure of realism in the performance of liturgical rites can help catechists to bring out the imaginative and affective dimensions of the liturgy and its relation to life. If Ambrose of Milan could speak in a picturesque manner about baptism as "the likeness of Christ's death and burial," it was because the rite directed catechumens to dip in the pool. If he could refer to the postbaptismal anointing with chrism as "the odor of the resurrection," it was because chrism was what its name says, namely a perfumed ointment.[60] If

60. Ambrose of Milan, *On Mysteries*, 6,29, p. 172.

Tertullian could inform us that the postbaptismal "unction runs on the body," it was because oil, which nowadays is used grudgingly, was poured abundantly on the head of the neophyte.[61] We frown today on excessive realism and graphic ritualization of the liturgy, but the other extreme can be disorienting and sometimes also distressing. The classic three drops of water at baptism, rancid chrism, and the white wafer called Eucharistic bread are some of the instances when liturgy turns tedious and stale. We cannot demand that catechists deliver vibrant and sensitive liturgical instruction if our celebration lacks the required ritual realism.

ACCULTURATION OR INCULTURATION?

It is clear from the examples involving the use of the typical editions that where the options they present have not been received by the particular ritual, the effort to garb catechetical instruction in cultural apparel will stop short of the aim to inculturate the form of catechesis. A fully inculturated catechesis presupposes an inculturated liturgy. If, on the one hand, the liturgy of the sacraments is grafted onto foreign language, rites, and symbols and, on the other, catechesis draws its material from the local community's life experience and culture, we should expect a breakdown in catechetical communication. The reverse, of course, is also true. An inculturated liturgical rite and a foreign-inspired catechesis will have the same unpleasant effect on the community. Depending, then, on the actual state of liturgical renewal in the local Church, catechesis will achieve inculturation or will have to settle for acculturation.

Acculturation of Liturgical Catechesis. We can expect acculturation to take place when the celebration of the liturgy, though in the vernacular, still follows the classical Roman pattern of thought, language, rites, and symbols, in short, when the liturgy of the local Church is lifted directly from the pages of the typical editions published by Rome. Catechesis has, however, already made progress in inculturation by adopting the language pattern of the audience and employing the rites, values, and images from the culture and life

61. Tertullian, *On Baptism*, 7,1; *FEF,* 177.

experience of the community. Nonetheless, these factors bring about a situation of discrepancy wherein the catechists will have to content themselves with the technique of dubbing the liturgy in with local equivalents in the hope of getting the message across. This scenario is not meant to downgrade the usefulness of acculturation. It is surely not the ideal way to renew and update liturgical catechesis, but often it is the only realistic thing to do, given the actual situation of the liturgy in a number of local Churches.

The following examples of acculturation will show the difficulty inherent in the method. At the rite of reception of children for baptism the typical edition directs the minister to sign the children on the forehead as an expression of welcome into the Christian community.[62] Though the English translation elaborates the Latin text by describing the sign of the cross as the Church's act of "claiming the children for Christ," the meaning behind the gesture is pretty much one of welcome.[63] Should catechists apply the method of cultural evocation, they would most likely encounter difficulty, depending on the cultural setting in which they teach, in explaining the sign of the cross as a gesture of welcome. The cross is hardly a symbol of the "great joy" the community experiences at the reception of children. In some cultures, a flower lei expresses festive welcome, while the sign of the cross on the forehead of a child has an apotropaic signification. It would not be a simple task to make the two worlds meet.

Catechists encounter in the rite of clothing the newly baptized in the white garment a similar difficulty.[64] Here the question is not so much the color of the garment, which need not be white if culture so requires, as the meaning it is expected to project. According to the typical edition, it is "the outward sign of Christian dignity." Catechists who explain to their listeners the meaning of Christian dignity by turning to their cultural tradition for enlightenment realize often enough that the baptismal cloth does not communicate the message. This is a common experience of catechists in those places where the baptismal garment is a piece of white cloth, if it is still white, looking

62. *Ordo baptismi parvulorum* (Vatican City, 1973) no. 41; *The Rites,* 1:199.
63. See A. Nocent, "Gli Ordines dell'iniziazione cristiana del Vaticano II," Anamnesis 3/1 (Genoa, 1986) 90–91.
64. *Ordo baptismi parvulorum,* no. 63; *The Rites,* 1:209.

like a napkin placed on the breast of each child. Furthermore, in modern society clothing of whatever shape or color does not indicate the dignity of a person but the peculiarity of the occasion. In traditional societies, the shape and color of the garment, though these are strictly observed, are not the only symbols of dignity. An eagle's feather, a bracelet or anklet, or an headdress shows the rank and dignity of a person in the community. Catechists are thus faced with the discrepancy between liturgical symbolism and cultural expression. Given the current form of the liturgy, such discrepancy is often inevitable.

Discrepancy is not confined to liturgical texts and rites. Liturgical furnishings have a share in the problem. The church building itself, which both theology and liturgy have so richly endowed with symbolism, becomes all too often a stumbling block for catechists. Is it the house of God, that is, a temple where God dwells, or is it the house of the Church, that is, "a building destined solely and permanently for assembling the people of God and for carrying out sacred functions?"[65] The answer, of course, is that it is both, though there are authors who tend to stress the latter.[66]

The architectural plan and style of a church reveal the theological concept underlying the edifice. Though in the early centuries, Christians, like the writer Minucius Felix, declared that "we have no temples and we have no altars," the shift from the theology of *domus Ecclesiae* to *domus Dei et porta coeli* came about rather quickly. If catechists are inclined to regard the church edifice as the meeting place of the Christian community, they would probably associate it with community halls, similar to the traditional *fale* of the South Pacific, or with the modern social halls of parishes and schools. But then the architectural setting of a Gothic church might have little to encourage its association with a community hall. Or catechists might turn for illustration to the conventional type of Buddhist or Hindu temples found in their region. But will they receive support from the architec-

---

65. *Ordo dedicationis ecclesiae et altaris* (Vatican City, 1977) ch. 2, no. 2; *DOL*, 1370.
66. See J. Boguniowski, *Domus Ecclesiae: Der Ort der Eucharistiefeier in den ersten Jahrhunderten* (Rome, 1986); P. Cobb, "The Architectural Setting of the Liturgy," *The Study of Liturgy* (London, 1979) 473–480; L. Chengalikavil, "La dedicazione della chiesa e dell'altare," Anamnesis 7 (Genoa, 1989) 101–109.

ture of our modern churches, which do not project, or are not meant to project, the image of a temple?

How about the altar? The double nature of the Mass as meal and sacrifice has given rise to a double name for the central piece of furniture, which is called "table" or "altar." The *Rite of Dedication of an Altar* has anticipated the difficulty and cleverly solved it by affirming that "the altar is the table for a sacrifice and for a banquet."[67] The statement is decidedly the product of a theological ingenuity designed to keep a healthy balance between the sacrificial and meal aspects of the altar. But it does not tell us whether the altar should look like an altar or a table. If catechists should decide to develop the aspect of the Eucharist as the family table around which the members gather together in intimacy, the reality of an imposing block of marble in the sanctuary would hardly fit the imagery.

The foregoing examples present the portrait of liturgical catechesis in situations where the liturgical rite remains foreign to the culture of the local Church. Liturgy and catechesis are merely juxtaposed. One thing is said in catechesis, and another is seen and heard in the liturgical celebration. The conclusion is evident: an inculturated catechesis presupposes an inculturated liturgy. Since "the authentic practice of the sacraments is bound to have a catechetical aspect," the ideal is for liturgical catechesis to obtain from the liturgy the instructional material that can evoke cultural experience. In the final analysis, the Church's obligation to foster harmony between catechesis and worship, or the work of evangelization and the exercise of Christ's priestly office, is heavily conditioned by another obligation, namely to inculturate the liturgy of local Churches.

Inculturation of Liturgical Catechesis. What then does inculturated liturgical catechesis mean? It means that the cultural pattern, system of values and symbols, and traditions of the local Church, which have already been absorbed through inculturation by the liturgy, are made available to catechesis. It implies that for their task of communicating the doctrine and spirituality of the sacraments in the context of the local Church's culture and traditions, catechists need not have recourse exclusively to outside materials. The liturgical rite already

67. *Ordo dedicationis ecclesiae et altaris*, ch. 4, no. 3; *DOL*, 1378.

possesses the elements that link the content of the sacraments with the life experience of people. On account of this, the liturgy itself has the upper hand in the way catechesis should unfold the Christian mystery. It is able to provide the material for catechesis and direct the course and method catechists should take.

But when the liturgy does not arm catechists with the kind of instruments needed to evoke cultural setting, they are frequently left to their own arbitrary devices. The effect on catechesis can be lamentable. The use, for instance, of true-life but often unrelated or irrelevant anecdotes, farfetched images, and remote social values does nothing but throw a heavy mantle of obscurity upon the nature and purpose of the sacraments. The doctrine or the substance of the sacraments is thus often lost in the maze of evoked personal experiences, which do not always attain the desired faith dimension of liturgical celebrations.[68] The inculturation of liturgical catechesis without the previous inculturation of the liturgy can exact a heavy penalty on the Church's work of evangelization.

The inculturation of liturgical catechesis will often consist in evoking cultural patterns, values, and social structures underlying the liturgical rites. The proposed *Misa ng Bayang Pilipino*, or Mass of the Filipino people, which we described early on, offers on several occasions concrete possibilities of applying cultural evocation in order to illustrate certain aspects of the Eucharistic celebration. In the Roman order of Mass, the presentation of the gifts is made, for greater structural clarity, at the start of the offertory rite. From the perspective of culture, however, gifts are normally presented to the host on arrival, not halfway during the celebration. If bread and wine and the other offerings are meant to be gifts, it seems that the appropriate moment to present them is right at the start of the Mass. Thus, the *Misa ng Bayang Pilipino* has transferred the presentation of gifts to the entrance rite. This would be a type of cultural pattern catechists could allude to in order to explain the value of coming to Mass with gifts to share.

Another ritual peculiarity of the *Misa ng Bayang Pilipino* is the Communion of the priest. The Roman order of Mass as well as the other liturgies in both the East and the West conform to a cultural

68. *Maturing in Christian Faith*, nos. 399–404, pp. 213–216.

system of precedence or ceremonial order. Thus the president of the assembly takes Communion ahead of the others. The practice expresses leadership and reverence for his office as ordained priest. In contrast, the *Misa ng Bayang Pilipino* follows a pattern of hospitality and parental concern, which is distinctive of the culture of several countries in the South Pacific. Hosts serve the guests first; in fact, they do not eat with them, and parents take their meal after the children have their fill. The message the *Misa ng Bayang Pilipino* wishes to communicate is not different from the one proposed by the Roman order of Mass, namely the leadership role and regard for priestly function. But by directing the priest to take Communion after everyone in the community has been served, the *Misa ng Bayang Pilipino* aims to situate the Eucharistic ministry of ordained priests in a local cultural setting. Catechists need no longer be apologetic about the Roman cultural system, which requires the observance of the order of precedence, or go through the pains of explaining that the first is really the last.

SUMMARY

In his apostolic exhortation *Catechesi tradendae*, Pope John Paul II sets the different conditions that must be faithfully observed when inculturating catechesis. In some way, these conditions sum up the main points that have been raised in this chapter. The relevant passages from this papal exhortation should be read, keeping in mind the distinction between the form and the content of catechesis. With respect to the form, the Pope affirms the superior role of catechesis in the dialogue the Church holds with the culture of every people: "We can say of catechesis, as well as evangelization in general, that it is called to bring the power of the gospel into the very heart of culture and cultures. For this purpose catechesis will seek to know these cultures and their essential components; it will learn their most significant expressions; it will respect their particular values and riches."[69]

In order for catechists to evangelize culture the Pope enjoins them to know, appreciate, and respect the particular culture in which they work. They should examine closely its constitutive patterns, deter-

69. John Paul II, *Catechesi tradendae*, no. 53, p. 667.

mine its most significant values and symbols, and show deep respect for its language and traditions. Not to do so would indeed be like preaching in the dark or proclaiming Latin liturgical formularies to an uncomprehending congregation. In a sense, the form and art of liturgical catechesis are akin to the form and art of liturgical translation. Catechesis, like translation, "must be faithful to the art of communication in all its various aspects, but especially in regard to the message itself, in regard to the audience for which it is intended, and in regard to the manner of expression."[70] This involves on the part of catechists an accurate perception of the social and spiritual situation of their audience. With respect to the manner of expression, catechists should keep in mind that culture is not a mere addressee of liturgical catechesis. Culture is meant to interact with catechesis and become part of its scheme, instructional material, and method. That is why catechists are required to possess a certain measure of familiarity with the local culture.

With regard to the content of catechesis, Pope John Paul II, as we have seen early on in this chapter, reminds us that the essential content or message of catechesis must not be isolated from the biblical culture, particularly of the New Testament, into which it was first inserted, nor, without serious loss, from the various cultures in which it has already been historically expressed down the centuries. The Pope very firmly states that the gospel message, which is the essential content of evangelization, "does not spring spontaneously from any cultural soil; it has always been transmitted by means of an apostolic dialogue."[71]

There are certain aspects of the content of catechesis that catechists should take into account in the process of inculturation as well as acculturation. Working on the premise that the essential content of catechesis "has always been transmitted by means of an apostolic dialogue," the Pope concludes that it cannot be communicated apart from the biblical setting of the message, particularly the cultural milieu in which Jesus lived. The patristic writings we examined employ biblical typology rather frequently in an effort to link the message of the sacraments with the biblical world. There are liturgical rites that

70. Consilium, Instruction *Comme le prévoit*, no. 7; DOL, 285.
71. John Paul II, *Catechesi tradendae*, no. 53, p. 667.

172

cannot, of course, claim any biblical origin; they have been borrowed from other cultural traditions or at least inspired by them. However, biblical typology is able to graft them onto the history of salvation. In some way they participate in the "apostolic dialogue." The Fathers, particularly Ambrose and Cyril of Jerusalem, have shown us that biblical typology is an indispensable companion of catechists.

The essential content of catechesis, which is likewise the chief message of the liturgy, has been transmitted to us through apostolic preaching. This fact should not, however, make us lose sight of its subsequent evolution after the apostolic age. It has grown in the course of the centuries through contact with the cultures in which the Church established itself. Pope John Paul II exhorts catechists not to discard in the process of updating the methods and material of catechesis the gains brought about by such contact. Catechesis is an historical reality. It should not make a sudden leap from the biblical world to modern times, bypassing the intervening twenty centuries. It is, as the Pope declares, "an experience as ancient as the church." The liturgical catechesis during the patristic age is always a point of reference, and so also, to some extent, are the medieval allegorical expositions, the Tridentine catechism, and the various catechisms that were produced from the time of Pope Pius X to the present.[72] Catechists have always something to learn from the past, even if some of its aspects, like allegory and moralistic approach, cannot obviously be included in the glorious annals of liturgical catechesis.

A final consideration touches on what Pope John Paul II has described as "an impoverishment of catechesis through a renunciation or obscuring of its message, by adaptations, even in language, that would endanger the 'precious deposit' of the faith, or by concessions in matters of faith or morals."[73] Inculturation, which is a type of translation, has always its dangers and risks, because no translation can adequately and fully represent the original thought. In the area of liturgical catechesis the danger can be attenuated if catechists take as their basic source and guide the typical editions of the liturgical

72. G. Cavallotto, "The Council of Trent and the Origins of Modern Catechesis," *GT*, 138–167; Idem, "Contemporary Catechesis from Pius X to Our Own Times," ibid., 168–187.
73. John Paul II, *Catechesi tradendae*, no. 53, p. 668.

books and, in the happy event that the liturgical rites are inculturated, also the particular rituals of the local Church. These books are not meant to stifle the renewal of catechesis but to guide the course of progress with the firm hand of liturgical tradition.